Jamaican Teachers, Jamaican Schools

Jamaican Teachers, Jamaican Schools

Life and Work in 21st Century Schools

Eleanor J. Blair
Western Carolina University

INFORMATION AGE PUBLISHING, INC.
Charlotte, NC • www.infoagepub.com

Library of Congress Cataloging-in-Publication Data

A CIP record for this book is available from the Library of Congress
http://www.loc.gov

ISBN: 979-8-88730-095-5 (Paperback)
       979-8-88730-096-2 (Hardcover)
       979-8-88730-097-9 (E-Book)

Copyright © 2023 Information Age Publishing Inc.

All rights reserved. No part of this publication may be reproduced, stored in a retrieval system, or transmitted, in any form or by any means, electronic, mechanical, photocopying, microfilming, recording or otherwise, without written permission from the publisher.

Printed in the United States of America

This book is dedicated to the Jamaican teachers who supported my efforts to teach, learn, and yes, collect data that would support my belief that they are extraordinary and deserve so much more than they currently receive for their efforts; the future of Jamaican education is in their hands. The Pandemic, and the changes it brought to our lives, has provided a context for new beginnings and new visions of what schools and teachers' work might look like in 21st century Jamaican schools. Given the opportunity, Jamaican teachers will create rainbows over their schools and participate in the production of something beautiful! There is much to do and time is so short. Walk Good *my sweet colleagues!*

Contents

Foreword—Beyond the Veil: Valuing the Nature of Teachers Work in Jamaica ix
Carmel Roofe

Preface: What's Love Got to Do With It? xiii

1 Jamaica: Begin With the End in Mind... 1
    Jamaican Culture, Identity, and Role of Diversity 1
    Jamaican Teachers 3
    Teachers' Work... 4
    School Reform 5
    Teachers' Work and Teacher Leadership..................................... 7

2 Jamaican Schools: Every Child Can Learn, Every Child Must Learn 13
    History of Jamaican Schools 13
    Social and Economic Challenges.. 16
    School Improvement and Reform 19
    Every Child Can Learn, Every Child Must Learn...................... 20

3 Jamaican Teachers: Walk Good 27
    Jamaican Teachers and Compensation 29
    Teacher Moonlighting in Jamaica 31
    Teachers' Work and the Voices of Teachers.............................. 36

4 Jamaican Teachers and Schools: 21st Century Teacher Leadership 49
   Teacher Leadership in Jamaica 50
   The Voices of Jamaican Teacher Leaders 59

5 Jamaican Teachers, Jamaican Schools: Disrupting the Narrative ... 71
   Teacher Leadership as Teachers' Work 72
   Teachers as Transformative Intellectuals 74
   Teaching as a Profession 75
   Teacher Leadership and the Pandemic 76
   Transformative Leadership in the 21st Century 82

References 89
Index 95

FOREWORD

Beyond the Veil

Valuing the Nature of Teachers Work in Jamaica

Carmel Roofe

Ellie Blair as the author of this compelling, thought-provoking book has courageously captured the nuances of teachers work in Jamaica while providing opportunities of hope for education in a country that is as complex as its history. The title aptly captures the contents of the book and is a great conversation starter for hope in a country where education and schooling is quite complex. Complex because of the colonial history that shapes how schools evolved and how teachers work is examined and articulated. Blair must be commended for the way in which language is used to provide the imagery of challenges experienced by teachers as they navigate their work and the opportunities presented to influence change while providing hope for teachers and their students. The book starts with Blair's story about her introduction to Jamaica, the country she now calls her second home and the work she has done with teachers. Each chapter

Jamaican Teachers, Jamaican Schools, pages ix–xi
Copyright © 2023 by Information Age Publishing
www.infoagepub.com
All rights of reproduction in any form reserved.

is grounded in her experiences, current policy changes, and empirical research within Jamaica. In this way Blair has guaranteed a unique contribution to the understanding of the past, present, and future work of teachers and Jamaican schools.

As a teacher educator in Jamaica I commend Blair for taking on this advocacy role and for highlighting the gains that have emanated from teachers work and for supporting teachers work in this manner. This is a crucial undertaking at a time when COVID-19 has heightened inequalities resulting in increased conversations about the need to reimagine education in Jamaica. I also am saddened by the harsh truths that Blair highlights about inequities that continue to exist in the structure and enactment of education in Jamaica. However, her quote—"We cannot let the exceptions determine policy and procedure for the masses"—reminds all who work in the field of education in Jamaica that we have a role to play in advocating for *all* so that all students and all teachers can achieve excellence, not just a selected few. Education is expected to provide a counter to conditions of inequality thereby giving everyone a fair chance. This book is a call to action for teachers and teacher educators to lead with bravery and purpose and to take our conversations beyond classrooms. This conversation is necessary in the public domain to educate about racism, colorism, and socioeconomic challenges that frustrate, and plague teachers work within the structure of schooling in Jamaica.

Jamaican teachers are well educated but the hierarchical structure of schools, the entrenched examination system, and the lack of resources often prevent teachers from exercising the agency that comes with that education. This is well documented in a chapter on Jamaican teacher leaders found in the volume produced by Blair et al. (2020). Another chapter by Chung Thomas et al. (2021) bemoans the accountability mechanisms that are implemented in Jamaican schools that stifle teacher's creativity and diminish teacher's autonomy rendering operations in school to reflect that of the colonial period. The narratives from teachers that Blair shares in this volume suggest that these issues continue to plague teachers work. Furthermore, based on the expressed narratives by school leaders when compared to teachers Blair notes the obvious disconnect between what teachers see and experience as the reality and what school leaders say. This disconnect also breeds mistrust and Blair highlights the evidence of lack of trust that shapes school culture.

Given the demands of education within the fourth industrial revolution, teachers' agentic role needs to be professionalized and elevated by school leaders and the central authority within the country. This needs to be addressed through the language used to speak about teachers work and the language used to implement changes in the system. To the outsider this may seem insignificant. However, given the oral nature of Jamaican society and the mistrust that exists this is critical. Teachers' agentic role needs to be elevated and spoken about positively by teachers themselves, school leaders, and the central authority within the country. This is one aspect of the culture that needs to be addressed if Jamaica is to truly provide a world-class education system. This is needed for collaboration and co-construction of solutions and to break the negative hierarchical structures of power as we envision the future of schools in Jamaica.

This book is definitely a conversation starter as it provokes one to look inwardly while reflecting on the status of teachers work in Jamaica. Blair has placed premium value on teachers work in a context where teachers work is undervalued. This is commendable and an example for other scholars involved in the work of teachers. Through this book we are reminded of the transformative role teachers play in the society and as such teachers' voices must be included in reform ideals that seek to address the root of the problem. This book sets the standard for discussions about 21st century schooling and deconstructs issues that are beyond classrooms; issues that clearly show the connection between teachers work, schooling, and the structure of society.

References

Blair, E., Roofe, C., & Timmins, S. (Eds). (2020). *A cross-cultural consideration of teacher leaders' narratives of power, agency, and school culture: England, Jamaica, and the United States.* Myers Education Press.

Chung Thomas, S., Roofe, C., Bailey, L., & Bennett, T. (2021). Accountability in schools in Jamaica as a mode of colonization: Threats to teachers' autonomy and students' creativity. In E. Blair & K. Williams (Eds.), *In handbook on Caribbean education* (pp. 64–89). Information Age Publishing.

Preface

What's Love Got to Do With It?

It wasn't love at first sight. In fact, my first visit to Jamaica was...well...complicated. I landed on the island with two small children and a husband in tow; I was sent by my university to teach Jamaican teachers who were enrolled in a program to earn their bachelor's degrees. My instructions were to simply teach an introductory educational foundations course that I had previously taught many times. Our first night in Montego Bay entailed a walk down the "Hip Strip" where I am certain we looked every bit the tourists who had just stepped off a cruise ship; we were accosted by myriad vendors proffering drugs, braids, bracelets, tours, and so on. We also quickly realized that commonly accepted safety protocols for small children in the United States were not in evidence on the island; no seatbelts in cars, exposed flood lights, and so on. A particular highlight was a lady offering to braid my daughter's hair for the $20 bill my daughter clutched in her tiny hands. Yes, she braided her hair, but only half of her head; the lady quickly looked at mom (me) and dad and said the other half would cost another $20. Indignant, we stomped off with a crying 5-year-old who only had half her hair braided. Great introduction to Jamaica, right? No problem "mon," the next day we found a local hair salon and took care of it. And actually, to be truthful, I didn't find a hair salon, the owner of the breakfast shop we found by the hotel saw my daughter's hair and offered to get it fixed. She grabbed my daughter and quickly

---

Jamaican Teachers, Jamaican Schools, pages xiii–xxi
Copyright © 2023 by Information Age Publishing
www.infoagepub.com
All rights of reproduction in any form reserved.

took her across the street for a repair; it was another $20, but we learned a valuable lesson (we were viewed as naïve and wealthy tourists), and hey, my daughter now had a full head of braids. We would be there for 2 weeks and so, trying to figure out how to buy diapers, feed picky eaters, and transport children around the island became a daily conundrum. As I said earlier, it was a complicated introduction to "paradise." Add to this chaos, my "new" teaching assignment. I entered class on my first day ready to teach familiar content; however, I had not been briefed regarding the fact that most of my "content" had no relevance to Jamaican teachers and schools. In a previous essay, I described my experience in the following way:

> Imagine my surprise when I entered the school where I would teach for two weeks and realized immediately that it did not look like any other school or classroom I had previously visited. The open-air classroom was hot and noisy with the whirling of ceiling fans, the walls were bare, desks were old and scuffed-up, the small classroom was filled to capacity with 40+ students, mostly women dressed in their Sunday best clothing; heels, hose, nice dresses and suits. And, did I mention that there was a goat munching on dinner outside the windows? It was a shock; I felt both confused and stupid, and totally unprepared to teach these wonderful students sitting in my class. Naively, I had thought that I was just going to Jamaica to teach an introductory education course that I regularly taught in the United States. As I began to attempt to teach, I realized that unlike my classes in the United States, there were no projectors or electronics, only a chalkboard and I had not packed chalk. I also soon learned, electricity was not always a constant; bad storms in this small Caribbean country often contributed to flooded roads that created travel problems, and yes, loss of power. Apparently, my astonishment and feelings of incompetence were visible on my face. Former students from that class would later tell me that they were surprised that I came back the second night for class; they were sure I would get on the next plane and leave. (Blair & Williams, 2021, pp. xviii)

My students, who were extraordinary, guided me gently in this "new" reality and I can only hope that I modeled how, as a teacher, to adapt "on the fly," but the first few days were spent revising the content of my course to fit the needs of Jamaican teachers while also trying to educate myself about the realities of Jamaican education. It was an arduous journey and I will be honest, at the end of the 2 weeks, I wasn't sure that I would ever return.

Yes, this "complicated" love affair with Jamaica began in 1993, and yes, I returned to Jamaica several times a year for 30 years. Jamaica became my other home and I became a "Jamerican." At this time, I have easily "returned" to Jamaica at least 100 times. I have probably taught a couple of thousand teachers. I've been told that there are few Jamaican schools that don't have at least one teacher who participated in our program and most of those students took at least one course from me. I have frequently visited schools in both urban and remote rural communities where I provided workshops and professional development to teachers anxious to learn and improve their pedagogical skills. I am humbled and filled with gratitude for the experience of walking amongst those teachers and their schools and can only hope that I gave as much to them as I received.

So, clearly, while it wasn't love at first sight, somewhere along the way, I fell in love with Jamaica. She became my other home; a place where I never ceased to feel like I made a real difference in the lives of both teachers and students. In Jamaica, I always felt grounded both professionally and personally; I grew and learned about race and social class and the impact of skin color in ways that would never have been possible in my privileged position at a predominately White university in the United States. On this island, I was the minority; I was the one identified by skin color first and the content of my brain...and heart...second. Respect and deference were easily given by the Jamaicans I encountered, but I frequently discerned a layer of distrust and skepticism regarding the relevance of work performed by "do-gooder" White folks sent to "educate" Jamaican teachers. Despite their independence gained from the United Kingdom on August 6, 1962, the impact of colonization is still an ever-present reality throughout Jamaican culture, but most definitely within the educational system.

Jamaicans understand the weight of oppression and racism and their efforts to fully embrace their independence and create schools and classrooms (and teachers) that are uniquely Jamaican are a part of the story I want to tell in this book. In subtle, but complex ways, Jamaican schools have regularly reinforced a sense of inferiority and a lack of value for the masses of children attending public schools. Working with limited resources in overcrowded classrooms, teachers and students experience firsthand the parameters of trying to accomplish seemingly improbable aims and goals; the vision is strong, but the road is full of potholes. The value of teachers and the work that they do has also been shaped by a general disregard for the allocation of sufficient resources to nurture and sustain excellence in education in all settings. Despite fierce expressions of patriotism and dedication to country and people, their cultural heritage is tainted by the threads of colonialism that still run through the fabric of their lives. For example, consider the disdain expressed for children speaking Patois (their native language) and the enforcement of a curriculum that replicates British educational practices; for example, drills, high stakes testing, and the streaming of children by ability and educational prospects. Fostering school programs that promote critical thinking, social justice, and inclusivity are not a priority among Jamaican educational leaders. Equally unlikely is a consideration that increased accountability doesn't have to translate exclusively into more tests. Alternative modes of assessment and teaching as well as challenges to the integrity of streaming and homework practices are not a part of the conversation on school reform, and yet, most teachers, given the opportunity, would love to explore the research on best practices in many of these areas. The status quo is seldom questioned and the allocation of resources maintains the sharp inequities between rural and urban schools as well as public and independent institutions. The prevalence of shift schools and schools that lack access to the most basic amenities—books, running water, technology, desks, well-trained teachers, and so on—are the vestiges of colonization and represent a willingness to accept that access to a *high quality* education is negotiable; shaped by social class and status, and most definitely, not a guaranteed right of any citizen. Schools I have visited in rural communities—the "bush" as Jamaicans refer to it—often have minimal resources: old and battered textbooks, computers that don't work, broken desks, and peeling paint. I am chagrined to remember making a comment to a teacher about the year-old calendar on her wall; she quickly responded that she had nothing else to put on the wall, no pictures, no posters, no educational materials. Urban schools can also be afflicted by a similar lack of resources, but also accompanied by violence among both students and teachers alike. I have often been warned against visiting schools in certain areas of Kingston because my safety cannot be guaranteed; the few I visited anyway were populated by teachers and students who seemed equally angry and frustrated. Teachers and students in these schools expressed a sense of hopelessness and discouragement about their circumstances; they know that no one cares and that the value put on their work is limited.

I struggle as I write these words because I know how proud Jamaicans can be. They are "hungry" for knowledge and desperately want to do better, be better. As I lament the educational challenges for both teachers and children, I also know that the island is rife with stories of individuals and their families who have focused on academic success as the one way to "lift" themselves out of poverty and despair. Families make great sacrifices to pull together the necessary resources to help their children go to the best schools, and frequently, they will send their children overseas to gain access to even greater educational opportunities. Previously, I met a gentleman, Solomon Gardner, who worked as the host or "beloved Keeper of the Mill and Half Moon icon" at the Sugar Mill restaurant in Rose Hall, Montego Bay for 53 years, who proudly told anyone who would listen his story of how he began working there as a teenager and never left; he has five children and several of them have advanced graduate degrees; all of them are accomplished professionals. His story resonates with families across the island; academic success is sacred. Even the taxi driver who has been driving me around Jamaica for 20+ years loves to brag about the educational success of his son; he works with this child daily and pushes him to achieve and gain access to the best schools. So, despite myriad educational problems, there are pockets of success, but I learned a long time ago that we cannot let the exceptions determine policy and procedure for the masses. Yes, some families find a way to provide educational opportunities when few are offered, but at the same time, there are large numbers of children who come from families living in abject poverty with parents who are ill-educated and unprepared to navigate an educational system that seems intent on maintaining an inequitable system that serves the few and ignores the many. For the families and children left behind and relegated to the lowest socioeconomic strata, the public schools may be their only hope. For teachers, this requires not only that they be skilled practitioners but also advocates, mentors, and guides.

Jamaican Culture

Jamaicans "understand" their culture and its uncomortable relationship with race, class and social justice better than most outsiders. George Graham (2012) wrote the following:

> Looking back on my Jamaican experience, it seems we are identified more by a class system than by racial labels.
>
> I know, "class system" sounds snobbish or worse. It has an unwholesome connotation, the implication of castes from which there is no escape. But I don't recall the Jamaican class system as being etched in stone. I recall the sons and daughters of domestic servants sometimes becoming wealthy doctors and lawyers, powerful politicians and bureaucrats, venerated members of the clergy, and so on.
>
> The education system, although admittedly inadequate, included scholarship opportunities that could provide a ladder for upward mobility. (Not enough, admittedly. But the opportunities are not as sparse today as they were in my time, and I am confident they will increase in Jamaica's next half-century as an independent nation.)
>
> Jamaica's class system is based on money, of course, but there are other criteria. These include European-based notions of etiquette and decorum, as well as education and the way people dress and speak. But there was something else, something that inherently defines the Jamaican concept of class.
>
> From what my mother taught me, it was "respectability." Respectable people lived by certain standards. They weren't "raw-chaw."

> Vulgarity, obscenity, drunkenness, arrogance, rudeness, slovenliness, idleness and "showing off" were considered signs of a "lower-class" upbringing.
>
> Another unspoken expectation of people in "our class" was decency.
>
> Decent people had integrity. Decent people didn't "take advantage." Decent people "did the right thing."
>
> Did all the members of Jamaica's "upper class" behave according to these standards? Of course not. Some abused their positions of privilege. (para. 5–12)

An emphasis on class rather than race defines one of the key differences between Jamaica and the United States, and at times, blurs attempts to discern how inequities are perpetuated. Social class embodies many characteristics but social class is also mediated by other important variables. One cannot ignore the biases that manifest themselves as issues associated with skin color (lightness or darkness), urban vs. rural, gender and sexual orientation as points of distinction that are quietly used to justify the inequities embedded into the system. It is often hard to understand many of these biases because they are hidden behind the belief systems embodied by the idea of *out of many, one people*. The "truth" about diversity, social class, and race is not immediately evident to the outsider and it is not one quickly revealed by Jamaicans themselves. It was only after working there for more than a decade that I really began to understand that the Jamaican understanding of race and class were much "richer" and multilayered than the American version. Winkler (1995) was my first introduction to the "lie":

> When it comes to colour, nothing in Jamaica is simple except the fairy tale often repeated that the island suffers only from class, but not from colour prejudice. This lie ranks as high in the pantheon of Jamaican delusions as the myth of the innocent American does in America. (p. 79)

Again, the tentacles of colonialism and the weight of oppression continue to shape views of race and social class in Jamaica. As such, talking about social justice, equity and equal access to education is impossible if one doesn't "tease out" the parts of that discussion that reflect deep-seated beliefs and values that have been a part of Jamaican culture for decades.

Jamaican Schools

I regularly tried to "push" my students to identify the issues that still "strangle" their efforts to redefine the process and product of education. Even among 21st century Jamaican teachers who are well-educated and prepared to take roles as school leaders, the constraints of previously defined notions about teachers' work and the status of teachers still "haunt" their efforts to guide the transformation of Jamaican schools. Several years ago, my Jamaican students read Henry Giroux's (2012) book, *Education and the Crisis of Public Values: Challenging the Assault on Teachers, Students, and Public Education*, and they delighted in talking about the "master" and serving the "master" in their schools. They understood the concept of a "plantation mentality" in a way that my privileged students in western North Carolina could not. My Jamaican students knew only too well the truths that echoed in Giroux's words:

> Teachers are being deskilled, unceremoniously removed from the process of school governance, largely reduced to technicians, or subordinated to the authority of security guards. They are also being scapegoated by right-wing politicians who view them as the new "welfare queens" and their unions as a threat to the power of corporations and values of a billionaire sponsored market-driven educational movement that wants to transform schooling into a for-profit investment rather than a public good.... Teachers are stripped of their worth and dignity by being forced to adopt an educational vision and philosophy that has little respect for the empowering possibilities of either knowledge or critical classroom practices. (pp. 1–3)

As they read these words and enthusiastically began to dissect the Jamaican system and the remnants of colonization, they had difficulty envisioning where they would find the power and autonomy to make changes occur. Sometimes, the product of critical analysis is frustration and resignation when one realizes the largeness of the effort to take apart a system and begin anew with a revised image. The reality, unfortunately, is that Jamaican teachers really do have little power and status, and my efforts to "stir the pot" and awaken teachers to another vision of teachers' work carried with it the responsibility of simultaneously acknowledging their current circumstances and helping them navigate previously untraveled roads. Even as I confronted these obstacles, I was comforted by the idea that I was planting a seed and that one day, these teachers would be the educational leaders in Jamaica. I regularly admonished my students to not forget where they came from; good words of wisdom for anyone navigating life's challenges, but particularly good ones for teachers climbing career ladders in strictly governed and conservative educational hierarchies. Ironically, when I go out to Jamaican schools to talk about teacher leadership, I encounter principals who want to share with me their efforts to build collegiality and professional learning communities and engage in action research, all good stuff and necessary for teacher leadership to thrive. However, this reality is disputed by the teachers I talk to in these schools. For example, in one school outside of Montego Bay, the principal was delightful and very enthusiastic about my work with teacher leaders; however, his teachers told another story. His teachers would pull me into closets or bathrooms to whisper in my ear that the principal does nothing to encourage partnerships with teachers, rather, he has his "favorites" that he supports while ignoring the vast majority of teachers in the school. In another inner-city Jamaican school, the teachers told me horror stories about their PhD trained principal who had never had a faculty meeting, and whose approach to leadership was to punish and threaten anyone who complained; a "carrot and stick" approach that relegates teachers to a semi-professional role that carries with it feelings of frustration and resignation with one's professional plight. The school was chaotic, students were openly bullying each other and teachers could only be described as demoralized. Not surprisingly, it was in that school that I was told that I could deliver a short workshop for the teachers, but I would not be allowed to talk to the teachers privately or in small groups and pictures of the school were not allowed. Jamaicans are a proud people, but I suspect the principal was afraid of public and professional reprisals that would impact her status and the security of her position at that school. I complied with her request, but later learned that the school is notable for its low achievement, chaos and high teacher attrition.

Twenty-First Century Educational Leadership

This book is a platform for telling a story; a story that is not unique or even a story that hasn't been told previously. However, I want this story, this book, to serve as a foundation for a larger conversation about the role that Jamaican teacher leaders must play in the growth and progress of Jamaican education in the 21st century. Jamaican teachers are brilliant, committed professionals. They are better educated than ever before in their history; and yet, they are still relegated to the status of semi-professionals. This book is an attempt to disrupt that narrative and promote a vision of teachers as leaders and front-line workers in the *re-forming* and *reframing* of Jamaican education. In my work, I often return to a simple idea that I encountered in Stephen Covey's (1982) work many years ago: "Begin with the end in mind"; if we can dream it, I believe that we can create it. I believe that if we want teachers to be educational leaders and decision-makers, we have to talk about the current status of the profession and begin to think about what the road to transformation looks like for 21st century Jamaican schools. As such, I want this book to be a part of the conversation; I want this book to both inspire and provide a platform for teachers to talk about their work, their dreams, and the future of Jamaican schools. Freire (2007) argued that "without hope there is no way we can even start thinking about education"

(p. 87). This book is put forth as a first step towards creating a context for hopefulness, and yes, promoting love as a feature of that hope...love of country...love of people. As such, it is possible to envision an island where dreams do come true for teachers and the children they teach.

1

Jamaica

Begin With the End in Mind

Never doubt that a small group of thoughtful, committed citizens can change the world. Indeed, it is the only thing that ever has.
—Margaret Mead

Jamaican Culture, Identity, and Role of Diversity

Writing a book about...and for...Jamaican teachers has been on my mind for years. As I approach the final chapter of my career, it represents a way for me to give back to them since they have so freely shared their lives and work with me for 30 years. As I will say throughout this book, Jamaican teachers are some of the hardest working people I know. They are educated, committed, funny, and extremely spiritual; the society as a whole is marked by the many contradictions brought about by the convergence of many diverse values and beliefs. Martin Luther King's (August 28, 1963), inspirational quote, "We may have all come on different ships, but we're in the same boat now" seems to apply beautifully to Jamaican culture. Understanding Jamaica and its people

Jamaican Teachers, Jamaican Schools, pages 1–12
Copyright © 2023 by Information Age Publishing
www.infoagepub.com
All rights of reproduction in any form reserved.

requires one to grasp the nuances of the diversity that defines it. The Jamaican national motto, *out of many, one people*, presents a noble goal, but it also obscures the fact that the Jamaican culture (and identity) is complicated by competing interests, both political and economic. Kirk Meighoo (1999) compared the Jamaican identity to the popular local cuisine, curried goat:

> Despite being Jamaica's second largest ethnic group, Indians have yet to be referred to as a meaningful or "real" Jamaican community in the same way that the Black, Brown, White, Chinese, or Syrian/Lebanese communities are. Indeed, Indo-Jamaicans largely exist in a situation where non-Indians who greatly outnumber them barely (and often only insultingly) recognize their existence. On the other hand, Indians do blend in quite naturally and inconspicuously in the Jamaican mélange...."Jamaicanness" must move from an obscuring, assimilative and reluctant plurality to a plurality that is celebratory, open and revealing. I propose that the present-day place of curry goat in Jamaican identity symbolize the direction for this future transformation. As curry goat is quite easily and readily seen as both Jamaican and Indian, so too must Jamaican identity itself be seen. (p. 43)

Just as identity is a complicated part of Jamaica, the spiritual aspect of Jamaican culture is also a dimension of Jamaican life that impacts most interactions, both formal and informal. I often tell students about my first teaching trip to Jamaica; I had prepared a lecture on the separation of church and state without realizing that I would be teaching in a Catholic school beneath a large crucifix and picture of Jesus. When I brought up the topic with my students, they told me that that was all nice for the United States, but no, there was no separation of church and state when it came to education and that was good with all of them. On my next trip, that topic was no longer a part of my presentation. Graham (2012) wrote the following about the Jamaican people:

> I cannot think of another society in which the Bible is so influential. Foreigners might think of Jamaica as some kind of hedonistic lotus land where Rastas in "dreadlocks" constantly play reggae music, dance suggestively and smoke ganja. But to me this is a false image probably created to lure tourists and sell records. The Jamaica I know is a churchgoing society. The Rastas I know spend more time talking religion than playing music. And the Rastas I know give and expect "respect." (paras. 14–16)

Clearly, I am not the only one who has taken note of this spiritual dimension of Jamaican culture and that spiritualism seems to imbue every aspect of the work in schools and classrooms. Each time I landed in Jamaica to teach, I was overcome with a feeling that I was returning home, and finally, doing work that really mattered. And so, their gifts to me have been immense.

Jamaican Teachers

Jamaican teachers give so much of their lives and souls to the work they do; and yet, even in 2022, I believe that they are neither paid a sufficient salary nor granted the respect and honor that they deserve. Recently, controversy raged in Jamaica over the 4% salary increase that was offered by the government (Wray, 2022). Many felt that Jamaican teachers were being greedy to request an increase in their meager salaries. A 2021 article in the *The Jamaica Observer* noted efforts of the Jamaican Teachers' Association (JTA) to dispel this notion,

> The teachers of Jamaica are painted in the public space as though we are craven, greedy, gluttonous, lazy, and worthless people who are just there to raid the coffers of the country, and that is not true," Jamaica Teachers' Association (JTA) President Winston Smith told the Jamaica Observer yesterday during an exclusive interview at his office.
>
> We need to dispel that rumour because that is not what teachers are about. As a matter of fact, we have been bent... to the point that our foreheads are now touching the ground. We are now left to be obliterated because every tissue, every muscle, every nerve, every capillary in our bodies have been stretched to the maximum," Smith said. (Hutchinson, 2021, paras. 2–3)

A 4% raise seems minimal when considering the already low salaries of most Jamaican teachers, but for some, the offer of anything was seen as a much needed reward for their hard work and effort. Smith went on to say in the interview,

> He said he does not get the impression that Jamaicans truly value education.... There has never been a single negotiation where the Ministry of Finance would look at teachers and say "We recognise your worth, we value your contribution, we see education as the pillars on which our economy can be built, so I am going to give to the teachers a decent, liveable wage," Smith said, noting that the JTA had asked for a 20 percent wage increase.... When we talk about teachers asking for an increase and the Government is going to look at us and say four per cent and nothing more, it is a wicked act. (Hutchinson, 2021, paras. 7–9)

These kinds of controversies highlight the needs and concerns of the average Jamaican teacher. The public disregard for teachers' requests for more pay and better working conditions reflects a pervasive negativity and disdain for the status of teachers and the important work they do. Many argue that as the profession is regularly upgraded through expectations for higher educational levels, accountability, and professional development, a natural outcome should be a rise in professional status, better working conditions, and compensation that measures up to the training, expertise and experience of the teaching force. It is always interesting that there are few arguments about doctor or lawyer salaries, but the public feels emboldened to critique efforts to improve working conditions and pay teachers a living wage. Perhaps, this thinking is embedded in notions about teaching as a calling and not a career choice that increasingly includes working long hours in unpredictable and challenging circumstances. While working conditions and compensation issues are serious deterrents to entering the profession, teachers persevere and these issues regularly show up as key reasons that teachers are dissatisfied and considering leaving the profession.

Teachers' Work

Teachers' work is the foundation of any meaningful change to the Jamaican system of education and schooling. Teachers know their students and they know the problems that afflict their profession and the impact that these issues have on the schools where they work. Increasing accountability and professional development will do nothing until we recognize the voices and work of teachers. When I talk to students about school improvement, they never mention the need for more accountability and random professional development. Most often, they are told *what* they need and then *given* mandatory training. I often tell my students that the problem with most "solutions" to school problems is that it is akin to the problem of weighing yourself on the scales every day; you can collect the data and even learn about weight loss and healthy eating but the data (your weight) will never change unless something substantial happens to affect all of the other variables that impact one's weight; for example, food, exercise, health, and so on. We can increase accountability and provide professional development (that is never clearly defined), but until we identify and attempt to address the "real" social and economic issues that impact schools, then more accountability and professional development will make no difference. Teachers who regularly experience a sense of powerlessness and hopelessness in their work are rarely good partners in school reform. Going to work every day in overcrowded and under-resourced schools is simply a reminder that despite the rhetoric to the contrary, no one really cares about what is happening to the masses of children on the island. Addressing social and economic issues that contribute to these problems is complicated and requires more than sound bites about school reform; we all know these facts but choose to ignore that reality when the sound bites get so much good press. Leaders who acknowledge the difficulties of implementing long-term solutions are not celebrated; the masses generally suffer from a perpetual case of attention deficit disorder, we want quick solutions to big problems and then we want to move on to something more interesting and popular. I often discuss the concept of "how we define the problem, determines the solution." If we spent more time critically examining the problems, the solutions would involve multilayer solutions where teachers' voices and work are central to the recommendations for reform. For teachers, the removal of barriers to professional growth and the development and creation of work environments that provide a sense of accomplishment, autonomy, power, and recognition are prerequisite to change. However, for many, this is a dangerous proposition. If I know anything after all of my years in academic circles, it is that those who have the power, seldom want to relinquish it or even share it. Any effort to promote teacher leadership and full professional status for teachers is often seen as an attempt to usurp the power of those who currently run the schools. I am not naïve; I recognize that while teachers may find these ideas exciting, many others will find them threatening. However, again... I return to the notion that if we can dream it, we can make it happen.

School Reform

In this book, I will frequently refer to the most recent report on Jamaican education that was published in January, 2022 and titled, The Reform of Education in Jamaica, 2021. The stated vision of this highly esteemed commission was the following: "Transforming our education system to enable all Jamaicans to fulfill their potential and contribute to Jamaica's development in the 21st century" (Jamaican Education Transformation Commission, 2022, p. 5). The report was prepared by a large and prestigious group of stakeholders who were representative of the wider community invested in educational outcomes;

> The report was produced through the engagement of a wide range of stakeholder's consultations both at the local and international levels. These include key stakeholders across the education system to include the Ministry of Education Youth and Information, agencies and departments of the ministry, schools, universities and colleges, the Opposition Spokesperson on Education, The Jamaica Teachers' Association, The Private Sector Organisation of Jamaica and other key international players. (Jamaican Education Transformation Commission, 2022, p. 11)

Most of the individuals who participated in the preparation of the report are affiliated with major institutions, schools, and organizations in leadership positions, only a few seem to be associated with Jamaican schools and none are identified specifically as teachers. Even more concerning within a context of building leadership capacity through the broad-based involvement of major stakeholders, there were no representatives from community groups or parents identified in the list of participants. Yes, the group was broad-based, but there were also strong political alliances that make critical decision-making complicated by the relational biases that are already in place. However, perhaps the more important questions should be: "Where are the voices of the teachers?" and "How do we shift the narrative to an acknowledgement that the system is floundering and teacher leaders may represent an important source of information not found in the data as well as a key resource for generating novel solutions to the problems inherent to Jamaican schools?" While the report frequently recognizes teachers as the linchpins that hold the system together, their response focuses on more accountability and professional development, issues already discussed in this chapter. A consideration of the status of teachers' work, working conditions, and salary issues that often lead to a lack of motivation and even attrition among teachers are not included in the recommendations. And thus, once again, the teaching profession does not change, schools suffer, and more importantly, learning and achievement are limited to the "chosen" few who have access to the best schools. Poor children in under-resourced, over-crowded schools continue to fail and teachers leave the profession. Education for the masses is not adequate and most certainly, it does not prepare them to be leaders or even productive citizens in a 21st century global economy. The Jamaican mantra, "every child can learn, every child must learn," is an effective public relations sound bite that obscures the ineffectiveness of schools and education across the island. Every child can't learn if their needs and the needs of their teachers are ignored and politicized to the point that change never occurs where it is needed most.

The report opens with a preface titled, "An Institution in Crisis." It provides a discussion of both the success and failures of the Jamaican system:

> The nation now faces two crises, one long in the making and partly within our control, the other an act of God and nature that threatens mankind globally. The first is our long struggle to overcome economic stagnation and social instability. As the Most Honourable Prime Minister, Andrew Holness, recently noted in his Emancipation Day speech, this crisis is deeply rooted in our violent and exploitative colonial past. There is now general agreement that the key to overcoming it is a well-functioning system of education. It is the primary engine of social and economic growth. For individuals it generates the increased income that promotes social mobility and well-being; it produces the skills, knowledge, and modes of thinking for our economy, polity, and social institutions needs; and it promotes the values that nourish our national culture, civil society, and stability. We have known this from the first day of our independence, and successive governments have, with admirable

bipartisanship, devoted increasing attention and resources to its development. There is no better indication of how highly we prioritize education than the fact that, today, Jamaica is among the top 20 percent of nations in the share of its national income and annual government budget devoted to this sector. (Jamaican Education Transformation Commission, 2022, p. 1)

The successes of the Jamaican education system are lauded; high enrollment of pre-primary children, access to education for a majority of children, establishment of top tier schools, athletic prowess, and so on; however, the failures are still profound and haunt efforts to have a larger impact on the general population. Only 10% of schools are considered a success and the inadequacies and inequalities that exist are unacceptable. The report states unequivocally that, "our greatest failure lies in the very success of placing the great majority of our children in schools where, sadly, the hopes of over a half are dashed by the end of their primary education from which they emerge illiterate and innumerate" (Jamaican Education Transformation Commission, 2022, p. 1). While some may read this book, and find it harsh, I remind the reader that these words come from a Jamaican Task Force; their assessment of the system is equally harsh, and more significantly, unforgiving.

Academic books examining Jamaican schools, and more importantly, the lives of teachers are in short supply. The popularity of Hyacinth Evans (2001) book, *Insider Jamaican Schools*, and her (2016) text, *Inside Hillview High School: An ethnography of an urban Jamaican school*, are evidence of the paucity of recently published literature that takes a critical look at the larger school culture that provides a context for teachers' work. While I believe that books on educational leadership generally, and the principalship specifically are important, these kinds of contributions fall short of the advocacy needed for a consideration of the impact on school improvement that would result from the expansion of the roles and responsibilities of teacher leaders. This book is intended to fill a gap in that literature and provide teachers and administrators and policy makers with a potential roadmap for school reform that includes teachers acting as teacher leaders in school communities that embrace constructivist principles of teaching, learning, and leading.

Teachers' Work and Teacher Leadership

Included in this text is recent research on teachers' work in Jamaican schools. Research completed in Jamaican between 2019–2022 on both teacher leadership and teacher moonlighting is used to "paint" a picture of the Jamaican teaching profession using the perspective of teachers to fill-out the description. Recommendations and suggestions are linked to this work. In this book, this research provides a context for discussions of teachers' work in Jamaican schools. This context is also informed by both the research and formal reports from the Ministry of Education, Youth, and Information as well as the Jamaican Teachers' Association (JTA). Additionally, this book considers the following five questions:

1. What does Jamaican teacher leadership look like?
2. How does Jamaican teacher leadership build the leadership capacity of Jamaican schools and why is that important?
3. What is the role of professional development in the evolution and reform of Jamaican schools?
4. Is Jamaican teacher leadership sustainable and essential in post-pandemic Jamaican schools?
5. What does the future look like for Jamaican teachers and schools?

Jamaican schools have been studied and discussed by myriad texts over the last 2 decades; however, a focus on teachers' work is missing from these studies. More recent studies have focused on important dimensions of Jamaican schools, but there have been no studies of teachers' work that have posited a vision of teacher leadership as a cornerstone of meaningful and sustainable efforts to reform both the schools and the teaching profession. It is not lost upon me that complicating this picture in 2022 is, of course, a consideration of the impact of a global pandemic on schools and teachers who are already struggling to gain access to the technology and acquire the pedagogical skills needed to participate in a 21st century digital world. When face-to-face learning is no longer an option, the digital divide is further exacerbated by the social and economic barriers that make it even more challenging for teachers working with low socioeconomic children and families who lack the technology needed to successfully participate in online teaching and learning. Teachers' work and the pedagogy that is the cornerstone of this work is seriously compromised by these kinds of issues. This book is not intended to provide answers, but rather to present information and questions that can be the foundation for critical discussion and dialogue among major stakeholders, and potentially provide an impetus for long-term sustainable and meaningful reforms.

Finally, the qualitative research in this book highlights the voices of teachers, and hopefully provides a platform for teachers to "see" themselves in this text as both mentors and advocates for novice teachers learning to teach, learn and lead. Disrupting previous narratives of teachers in semi-professional roles challenges each of us to consider where the teaching profession has been, where it is today and what it could look like in the future. If teachers are important to making Jamaican schools more successful, and most reports from the various task forces acknowledge the importance of teachers, then thinking about teachers' work differently and within a context of teacher leadership may be the first step to defining what a 21st century Jamaican teaching profession will look like and how it can function as the foundation for "real" school reform. It is hoped that teachers will see this book as affirmation of their values and beliefs and confirmation that there is a role for them to play in school reform that is much bigger than simply being accountable for test results and participating in more professional development.

This book presents a review of key literature and research on teacher leadership and applies it to the Jamaican educational system in order to discuss what the reports do not discuss; how teachers are essential to any meaningful reform of schools. It is naïve to discuss teachers' work in terms of accountability and professional development and ignore the vast array of variables that shape the unsatisfactory, and frequently unsafe, working conditions faced by both urban and rural Jamaican teachers. The conditions of teachers' work must change; teachers must have increased autonomy in their work lives if they are to take their rightful places as educational leaders working to improve the educational futures of Jamaican children. Regularly, I refer to the idea that "how we define the problem, determines the solution." If teacher feedback is not an intrinsic part of defining the complex nature of pedagogical issues and problems then the solutions will never adequately address the most deep-seated, and often, complicated issues that are facets of teachers' work.

Professional development and accountability are crucial to teachers' work, but both of those variables are frequently disconnected from the social and economic variables that shape what goes on in individual schools and classrooms. Teachers must participate in the asking of questions prior to formulating answers and prescribing solutions that only do one of two things; address the "red herrings" that have captured the attention (and imaginations) of public figures or provide short-term answers to long-term questions. Indeed, teachers already know their students' needs and recognize that, "how we define the problem, determines the solution"; teachers are ready and willing to begin the difficult task of articulating "real" solutions to "real" problems. These problems are seldom easily defined and most often have multiple layers of complexity. If we continue to define the problems in Jamaican schools as issues that can in many ways be considered symptoms of broader more endemic social issues then the solutions will only be band-aids that temporarily provide the appearance of relief. Solutions that have a singular focus will never be sustainable and the problems will only reemerge in another guise at another time. In the meantime, we lose the momentum of relevant school reform efforts, and perhaps, more tragically, we continue to see an exodus of teachers from the island. If teachers represent one of Jamaica's most valuable resources, efforts to address issues related to teachers' work are paramount and must remain in the national conversation until positive, forward motion is achieved. I believe that the emergence of new roles and responsibilities for Jamaican teachers in Jamaican schools will provide the "fuel" for this kind of revolution.

Solutions that ignore the research on best practices and don't provide a space for application to a uniquely Jamaican system of education are doomed to failure and frustration. Post-colonial practices must emerge that seek to redefine an educational system that celebrates the unique talents and gifts of Jamaican children in ways that translate to the curriculum and accountability practices. Teachers working as intellectuals with the power and status to initiate and apply research to Jamaican schools (both urban and rural) are the only way that meaningful, sustainable change will begin to emerge. All of this is possible if only teachers were not relegated to the sidelines as semi-professionals who cannot be trusted to make the important decisions. So-called experts who may be great leaders but are removed from the front-line dilemmas of schools are seldom equipped to deal with pedagogical issues as well as social and economic crises that continue to upend the progress and product of education and schooling.

Fundamentally, there has to be a vision if we want to change; a dream about what the future can look like under the best of circumstances. Without a vision, we are akin to a ship without a compass. While some will argue that dreams may present dangerous expectations for unreachable goals; I don't think that is true. Without dreams, there is always the prospect that one will descend into a sea of despair that makes it appear that change is not possible and that the acceptance of mediocrity and failure are acceptable and even rational. In 2010, the Vision 2030 Jamaica National Development Plan: Planning for a secure and prosperous future was published. The plan sets out a vision for the future tempered by the realities that define the present. The vision sets out 4 national goals that lead to 15 outcomes for Jamaica's secure and prosperous future. The goals are the following: "1. Jamaicans are empowered to reach their fullest potential, 2. The Jamaican society is secure, cohesive and just, 3. Jamaica's economy is prosperous, and 4. Jamaica has a healthy natural environment" (Planning Institute of Jamaica, 2010, p. 16). The report acknowledges the challenges facing the country in 2010:

- inadequate health personnel, infrastructure, and equipment;
- poor performance of learners, especially boys, at different levels of the education system;

- need for better trained education personnel;
- inadequate parenting;
- discrimination against persons with disabilities;
- inadequate support for the vulnerable in the society;
- not enough attention to positive values such as truthfulness and respect for each other;
- inadequate resources for the development of culture and sport.

(p. 18)

Poor student performance especially among boys, the need for better trained education personnel and inadequate parenting are the key challenges identified that impact educational outcomes. The vision for education is defined by a desire to create excellent learning environments that address the needs of all children and world class training for teachers. The plan delineates the things that will be done to ensure access to a high-quality education for all children; however, it falls short in plans for supporting the training and development of world-class teachers. Consistent with the 2021 Jamaican Education Transformation Commission Report, educational accountability is touted as part of efforts toward school improvement, but again, teacher training and professional status are not referenced. Indeed, it seems that key issues associated with education and schooling generally are minimized, and yet, the development of strong schools that assure access to a world-class education is central to a secure and prosperous Jamaica. Without an educated citizenry and well-functioning schools, nothing else in the plan is achievable at the levels discussed in the vision. As is true with most reports, Vision 2030 initially got a lot of attention, but discussions of its stated goals and strategies have diminished. Again, a vision is needed to construct our dreams, but a vision has to be informed by a realistic assessment of where we are and seek to identify *all* the variables that will contribute to the success of goals and strategies. Albert Einstein is credited with saying, "If I had an hour to solve a problem I'd spend 55 minutes thinking about the problem and five minutes thinking about solutions." Too often, the reports that emanate from the various government task forces are solution oriented without spending the time needed to think about how we define the problems.

As stated earlier, this book is a labor of love grounded in hope; I hope that this book will promote change-oriented discussions and provide a roadmap for defining how to overcome current obstacles to successful school reform. Again, my affection for Jamaica is grounded in a profound admiration for the commitment and work I see among its educators, but woven within that tapestry is also something bigger, something spiritual that I never failed to feel on each of my trips to work in Jamaica. Jamaicans share a sense of community and optimism that is an extension of their faith in God; Jamaicans believe that regardless of how difficult the road, the destination is worth it. At times, I was appalled by the circumstances of teachers' work, but my students never seem shocked by the grim realities of many schools and communities. They believe that it is possible to not only survive, but to thrive despite the benign neglect so often offered by those in powerful positions. Even as I talked to them about the inequities associated with class bias, racism, oppression, colonialism, and diaspora specifically and social justice generally, they often saw few solutions to their plight, but were still more than willing to dissect their experiences and try to understand the foundation for change and transformation. As much as I wanted to see anger and outrage and demands for immediate change, I didn't see those things, but rather, I saw groups of teachers who were still committed and passionate about the formidable work in front of them. And this, my readers, is why I remain equally committed to helping tell their story; it is important and I am simply a vessel for this discussion with a broader audience. In this book, I hope to merge reality with a vision of possibilities. And in this vision, I want to present myriad opportunities to consider how my beloved "other home" can find a plan or a road that leads to achievement of educational prominence in the Caribbean, and even perhaps, on a world stage through the highest caliber teachers and schools doing what they do best; collaborating and supporting one another and being true to the mantra, *out of many, one people*. After reading this chapter, envision the changes that would be necessary to *begin with the end in mind*. Consider the following questions:

1. What are the implications of *out of many, one people* for the reform of public education? How does this ideology function in practical application; for example, the curriculum, resource allocation, assessment? Who will define what an education looks like that is appropriate for "one people"? Is universal access mediated by a concern for equitable resources, content, and quality? What social goals and purposes are part of a vision for "one people" in education?
2. If all social and economic barriers were removed, what would Jamaican schools look like? What would happen to shift schools? How would teachers' work be restructured? What resources would be required? How could resources be re-allocated?
3. If teacher leadership was the norm in Jamaican schools, how would this function in conjunction with the Ministry of Education, Youth and Information? Would there be a re-alignment of leadership? What would that look like? Propose a new hierarchy within the larger system of a centrally organized system of public education.

2

Jamaican Schools
Every Child Can Learn, Every Child Must Learn

> *We don't want a place at the table, we built the table.*
> —Bettina Love 12/05/2020
> Initiative for Race Research and Justice, Vanderbilt University

History of Jamaican Schools

Jamaican schools have a complex history that is mediated by the impact of British colonialism and the long-anticipated liberation and emancipation that came with independence in August, 1962. The 2004 Task Force on Educational Reform described the historical precedence for public education,

> Public education in Jamaica dates back to 1835, when Jamaica, a British colony, received financial assistance under the Negro Education Grant, for the education of the formerly ex-slaved populace. Several religious bodies were given the responsibility for the administration of the grant while the colonial legislature gave the educational directives. (Ministry of Education, 2004, p. 41)

Jamaican Teachers, Jamaican Schools, pages 13–25
Copyright © 2023 by Information Age Publishing
www.infoagepub.com
All rights of reproduction in any form reserved.

In a system, not so different from the United States, two types of schools emerged; elite, and often private schools, for the wealthy and publicly funded schools that served the working classes. Student expectations and curriculum were quite different in each category of schools; wealthy children were being prepared for higher education and leadership positions while working class children were preparing for blue-collar, service-type jobs. In this way, schools became the gatekeepers of education and social mobility was closely tied to educational attainments. What emerged was a two-tiered form of education that persisted until independence in 1962,

> Education was given full responsibility for education and with Independence in 1962, came the challenge of introducing new policies and programmes, and commencing the process of reforming the education system.
>
> The common articulated vision was "Education for All." A clear, long-term development programme aimed at providing the best education the country could afford was embarked upon. A new curriculum provided a wide range of post-primary courses to thousands of children, with an emphasis on technical and vocational education in preparation for the world of work. These changes were complemented by the expansion of the tertiary level including the teacher training colleges.
>
> During the first 15 years of Independence, universal access to primary education was achieved; more than eighty percent of children were enrolled at the lower secondary level (Grade 7–9) and almost 60% at the upper level. Approximately 83% of the teachers were college trained. Government absorbed the operating cost of almost all the high schools owned by Denominations and Trusts under a grant-in-aid arrangement. This facilitated an increase in the flow of children of working class parents into traditionally elite schools. The Common Entrance Examination functioned as the screening mechanism in a highly competitive selection process. Students who were selected went to traditional high schools the rest flowed automatically to New Secondary Schools, resulting in an institutionalised two-tiered system—one for the upper and middle class and the other for children of the masses. (Ministry of Education, 2004, p. 42)

Today, Jamaica is the largest English-speaking island in the Caribbean. It has a population of approximately 3 million people. The population is diverse and represents the convergence of people of African, European, East Indian and Chinese heritage. Characterizing their optimistic and collaborative view of this diversity is their motto, "Out of many, one people" or in another popular soundbite, "one love, one heart, one Jamaica." Despite this diversity, Jamaica is a complex country where race, economic, and social issues dominate political discussions and often lead to heated arguments about the appropriate aims and purposes of various endeavors.

These disagreements are never more poignantly expressed than in critiques of the educational system and attempts to reorganize and re-vision the process and product of public education in the various task force reports that regularly appear to document both the failures and successes of Jamaican schools and the teachers. In the 2004 Task Force on Educational Reform—Jamaica—A Transformed Education System documented both the failures and success of Jamaican schools:

- National curricula and standardized testing programmes at the primary and secondary levels.
- The provision of a space in public primary level schools for every Jamaican child 6–11 years, as well as a space at the secondary level for more than 70% of children 12–16 years.
- The more than 22,000 teachers, some 80% of whom are trained, who continue to provide yeoman service, despite the many challenges.
- The more than 12,000 persons who provide voluntary service by serving on boards of management of schools.
- The thousands of parents who support schools through Parent/Teachers Associations and other community groups.
- Other support programmes such as School Feeding and Textbooks.
- The tremendous partnerships between Government, Churches, and Trusts in realizing a capital investment in the educational plant worth over $200 billion dollars at replacement value. (Ministry of Education, 2004, pp. 3–4)

However, the task force also noted the ongoing failures of Jamaican schools,

While celebrating these achievements, we shared the concerns regarding the poor performance at all levels of the system. For example:

- The proportion of children entering school ready for primary level education.
- The literacy rate at Grade 4
- Performance on the Grade Six Achievement Test
- Performance in the CSEC examination, especially in English language and mathematics. (Ministry of Education, 2004, p. 4)

Access to knowledge and literacy is a fundamental part of any discussion of liberation and emancipation, and as such, it has been a part of the educational tapestry of Jamaica for many decades. If students lack access to basic literacy and mathematical skills, it is unlikely that they will be able to function in 21st century society as full-functioning adults with livelihoods and families and the ability to contribute in meaningful ways to a community. And yet, this is the reality for many Jamaican children, the schools are broken and without access to personal resources, they are left to flounder in schools that provide an education that is minimal and inadequate under any circumstances.

Social and Economic Challenges

Through the years, as an outsider, it has been impossible to not be struck by the social class dichotomies that dominate the Jamaican educational landscape. While independence provided an opportunity to forge a new educational path, the challenges of creating a system of education that is uniquely Jamaican have been daunting. It was far easier to replicate the British system of schooling and make small changes along the way. However, the failures of this system are well-documented and mounting. For the vast majority of children, schools have not provided a mechanism for social mobility but rather replicated a social class system where many families are left behind in poverty with few opportunities for advancement. The result has been illiteracy, school attrition, and unemployment that frequently leads to large segments of the population who manage to survive as unskilled laborers or in worst case scenarios; as street vendors, sex workers, or drug dealers. Individuals often live on the streets or in substandard housing and violence, petty thefts and assaults occur with a high level of frequency. While education is not the only answer to these kinds of issues, adequate schools and good teachers are a source of hope for many people looking for a way to improve their circumstances.

As a frequent visitor to Jamaica, I know only too well the dichotomies that exist between schools that serve the more affluent and those that cater to a less privileged population. Independent schools that serve students from a middle to higher socioeconomic background offer a curriculum and teachers that would be satisfactory in any part of the world; the classrooms are colorful and well-resourced with eager and engaged students. I have also seen classrooms and schools in less-privileged communities that lack running water, books, computers, and even toilets for students; classrooms are shabby and over-crowded with broken desks and dirt floors. In these schools, issues related to indiscipline, bullying, and low attendance are rampant. Not surprisingly, there is a correlation between achievement and resources; highly resourced schools show greater academic gains and lower resourced schools struggle to meet minimal standards. I believe Theodore Sizer noted this correlation in his book, *Horace's Compromise*, when he argued, that with regard to American schools, one only had to know the social class of the school population to understand resource allocation and student achievement as well as a host of other predictors of academic success (Sizer, 2004). The same truth exists in 21st century Jamaican schools. While the correlation is complicated by many variables, the outcomes are clear; some students will succeed while many others will leave school illiterate and lacking even the most basic academic skills. The challenges (lack of resources, overcrowding, poverty) that ultimately give birth to inequity and lack of access to equal education make it hard to characterize Jamaican education with summary statements. Despite the mantra, *out of many, one people*, Jamaican education is a tapestry that is riddled with contradictory stories of people who lifted themselves up from poverty to succeed and the masses of children who were unable to do so. Social justice as a concept is noble; however, the realities are not hidden from the average Jamaica; Graham (2012) wrote the following:

> Undoubtedly Jamaica's class system is unfair. Without question, people born into Jamaica's underclass have to struggle much, much harder to achieve economic and social success than the lucky few who are born to privileged parents. Sadly, many decent, respectable people find themselves mired in poverty and subjected to indignity. And usually, these "sufferers" belong to the predominantly black underclass. (para. 23)

Change, reform, and even transformation are not easy tasks, but they require frank and honest discussions of the barriers to social justice, both social and economic; there are no easy fixes. Complex problems require complicated... and thoughtful solutions that involve *all* major stakeholders. Even in the worst of schools, I still find teachers and students showing up and attempting to participate positively in educational endeavors. Hope and optimism in these settings are scarce, and yet, I don't find anger, but rather, resignation.

It is profound that in 2013, Heremuru characterized Jamaica as a "failed state" and

> rather than on the brink of being labeled a successful nation... It is a country that continues to struggle in its attempts to move away from a past and a present marred by economic crisis. It is a country whose politics continue to shape the environment in which educational organizations operate. Those challenges, coupled with increased scope and speed of globalization and technological advancements have contributed to the creation of an education sector that is not viable for sustaining the economy. (p. vii)

Heremuru (2013) describes the remnants of this colonial past in the following:

> Decades after colonization, Jamaica's education system carries remnants of its colonized past. Meaningful reform strategies remain unattainable, Noel, a Jamaican educator puts it this way "we implemented half-measures-changes that were not fundamental enough to make a real difference and so doomed to half-success" (Noel, 2009, para. 10). Access to quality education remains largely determined by societal class. An examination of the resources available to students in traditional high schools and private

schools in comparison to those of most upgraded high schools and junior high schools shows great discrepancies. The former are far often better resourced. (p. 17)

Hyacinth Evans (2001) ended her book, *Inside Jamaican Schools*, with the following:

> Addressing inequality and the practices by which it is created is urgent in a postcolonial society which was founded on inequality, and which placed (and still places) more value on some cultural traditions, and social and racial/ethnic groups than on others. The legacy of this history is evident in the problems of identity, and a lack of self-confidence and self-acceptance among a significant number of children and young people in our schools and in the wider society. The existence of unequal and stigmatizing practices in a postcolonial society demands a radical reorientation and new consciousness on the part of the school and of individual teachers. Since the 1960s, the Ministry of Education and Culture has given priority to increasing access to education for a wider cross-section of Jamaicans, changing the curriculum to provide more quality education, and, in recent years raising the level of achievement of students. Very little attention has been paid to the internal workings of schools and the processes by which and through which education is accomplished. (p. 150)

Problems with diversity and indiscipline are constant reminders of the great divides that characterize education and schools in Jamaica. Again, Anthony Winkler (1995) in *Going Home to Teach* introduced me to the concept of race in Jamaica:

> Americans see colour strictly as a consanguineous and physical quality: it is to them so much a matter of blood that a pint inherited from a great-great-great black ancestor is enough to classify anyone as black no matter how white he may look. Jamaicans, and West Indians as a whole regard colour as inseparable from manners, behavior, background, education, and culture—that whole constellation of traits the Englishman once labelled "breeding." This fundamental and deep-rooted difference between Americans and Jamaicans, and possibly all Caribbean peoples, may in part be responsible for the antagonism that some say exists between American blacks and blacks from the West Indies. (p. 80)

Winkler's (1995) discussion of race in Jamaica is consistent with previous references to the ideas of George Graham. The inequities are severe and the distinctions between the haves and the have-nots are sharp. Indiscipline was a term that confused me when I initially came to Jamaica; it seemed to refer to any form of misbehavior but was also related to race in ways that I was not familiar with in America. Winkler (1995) described it as "unculturedness, and general ill-mannerliness" and equated it as evolving "intact into our cultural soul from the earliest slavery days when a black skin signified captivity and barbarism" (p. 89). The pervasiveness of this term in Jamaican educational discourse cannot be denied, "Indiscipline is the one word that most Jamaicans, on a free association test, would equate with blackness. Jamaicans of all walks of life seem to spend a lifetime bemoaning indiscipline" (p. 89). And yes, most task forces charged with school improvement in Jamaica note the issues associated with various forms of behavior; for example, violence, assaults, petty theft, and bullying. Fighting among students and assaults on teachers are daily occurrences in some schools and make efforts to focus on pedagogical issues a challenge.

School Improvement and Reform

School improvement continues to be the goal of various reform efforts; for example, the recent release from the Jamaica Education Transformation Commission, The Reform of Education in Jamaica 2021—The Report. The report documents that

> the education system is one of the largest institutions in Jamaica. The Ministry of Education, Youth and Information (MOEYI), with its approximate eleven agencies and 7 regional offices, employs over 25,000 teachers who educate nearly 580,000 students in over a thousand educational centers. Jamaica provides access to education to nearly all children of pre-primary and primary ages and to the majority of those in the secondary school cohorts 18 and under. (Jamaican Education Transformation Commission, 2022, p. 24)

And yet, despite decades of efforts to define and create a uniquely Jamaican education system, the outcomes are disappointing. The report found, "Although Jamaica has a good record in providing near universal access to primary school, it has failed to educate at the most basic level a substantial proportion of its children. Exam results in 2019 indicated that at the end of 6 years of primary schooling 59% were failing mathematics, and 45% were failing in language arts. Jamaica's tepid economic performance over the past half century, not to mention its related chronic social problems, can in good part be attributed to its learning crisis" (Jamaican Education Transformation Commission, 2022, p. 19). And yet, the recommendations of the report are the following:

> Five fundamental principles motivate our objectives and recommendations for the reform of Jamaica's education system: organizational coherence in the governance of education, internal and external systemic alignment in its functioning, a pedagogic transformation focused on the instructional core

of learning as a collaborative process, a revision of the curriculum grounded in the complementary learning of STEAM (Science, Technology, Engineering, the ARTS, and Mathematics) and SEL (Social and Emotional Learning) disciplines, and the vigorous pursuit of equity. (p. 19)

The ways in which Jamaican schools have reinforced a sense of inferiority and a lack of value for the masses of children attending Jamaican public schools have occurred in subtle ways, but the imposition of lowered academic standards that don't include a STEAM and SEL focus are just a few of the ways that schools are failing to prepare Jamaican children to become 21st century global citizens. Regimented academic practices that focus on drills, rudimentary knowledge, tracking, and high stakes testing and a lack of acceptance of Patois as a legitimate mode of communication are just a few of the ways that children internalize lower expectations for success. Critical, creative thinking that challenges the status quo and promotes social justice is not a part of forward-thinking efforts among Jamaican leaders. And before anyone challenges these statements, I ask you to consider the prevalence of shift schools and schools that lack access to the most basic amenities; books, running water, technology, desks, well-trained teachers, and so on. If children are valued, if *all* children are valued, educational resources will be allocated for the provision of an education that meets minimal 21st century standards and teachers, parents, and educational leaders should be demanding answers to questions regarding who gets limited resources and who does not.

Every Child Can Learn, Every Child Must Learn

Jamaica prides itself on educating all children, "Every child can learn, every child must learn," is the mantra of the Jamaican Ministry of Education, Youth and Information (MOEYI). In the 2004 Task Force on Educational Reform—Jamaica, this vision was expanded to be the following:

> Each child can learn...Every child must
> Education is everybody's business
> Education is an Attitude. (Ministry of Education, 2004, p. 29)

No one can disagree with the importance of this commitment. In fact, the 2004 task force report states, "The first step towards transforming the education system is the agreement by all stakeholders on the philosophy that will guide every decision made" (Ministry of Education, 2004, p. 28). And yet, regularly, children are not educated; illiteracy rates and school attrition continue to be high among the most vulnerable students. And yet, even with independence in 1962, Jamaican educational policy-makers and leaders still replicate a system of education that treats teachers as semi-professionals, at best, and sustains schools that are over-crowded and under-resourced. While most of the population speaks Patois for everyday transactions, the schools mandates the "Queen's English" in a country with no queen. According to some Caribbean linguists, only 1% of Jamaicans speak English as their first language. The rest speak "patois," "Creole," "Afro-English," or "Jamaican" as it's variously known. Now the government is facing demands to include protection for patois speakers in the constitution (Turriff, 2002). Winkler (1995) noted the contradictions in his discussion of Manley's Regime in Jamaica,

> At the school, for example, I was at first astonished to hear the teachers in the staff room freely talking in patois. When you think about it, this is as it should be, since patois is the language that all Jamaicans speak in the crib. But in the 1950s the Englishman still had Jamaica squarely in his grip and many of the generation that reared us were convinced that patois was an infra-dig and ignorant tongue. Patois was the condescending language you might use on a servant or a menial, but it was unthinkable that two professional Jamaicans conversing in public should lapse into it. Yet under the Manley regime patois had gained widespread acceptance as the language of informal talk between Jamaicans, even as a symbolic badge of belonging, and in the daily exchanges between teachers in the staff room, the foreign staffers who could not understand but speak it seemed sorrily misplaced. (p. 91)

The use of patois as an acceptable language for transactions is still mired in controversy, and yet, the ironies are palpable. A transformation of education inclusive of the roles and processes within a system that begins with challenges to the remnants of colonization are not a part of any report or task force on Jamaican education.

What if we began by asking pedagogical questions centered on curricular issues; for example, the philosophical values and beliefs undergirding decisions about what and how to teach, roles of teachers and learners, and more importantly, the role of assessment in educational data collection and planning for instruction. Replicating the formerly British system of education reproduces social and economic class biases and relies on a strict adherence to streaming and corporal punishment. Critical questioning of the tenants that inform these decisions can provide an opportunity to not only "think outside of the box," but also to initiate an effort to define what is uniquely Jamaican about the Jamaican system of education and how the needs of Jamaican students may require a different kind of school and classroom experience. Attempting to break down the meaning of "every child can learn, every child must learn" can be the beginning of a process of identifying why every child is not learning in Jamaica and what kinds of steps would need to occur to make that happen. In Johnson's (2022a) essay, *Every Child Can Learn, Every Child Must Learn, Part I*, she discusses the hypocrisy of this ideology:

> Then rides in the Ministry of Education on its white horse to "save" the day. It rides to the theme song, "Every child can learn. Every child must learn." The rhythm and words of this song is pleasing to the ears and very catchy, but when we pause long enough to observe what is happening behind the music, can we really "hear" and see the "vibrations" in the schools?.... The Ministry of Education clearly states that "Every child can learn. Every child must learn." I totally agree with this, but I am still left with two questions. "Learn how and learn what?" How do we show ALL our children that they CAN learn? How do we ensure that ALL our children learn? It has been said that "Every student can learn, just not on the same day, or in the same way." (paras. 6–10)

Answers to these kinds of questions could serve as the impetus for a defining what Jamaican education could and should look like in the 21st century as well as a consideration of teachers' voices as an essential part of the response.

Concerns about how the Ministry caters to *all* children must include adequate resources and services to address learning differences and difficulties that result from social and economic disparities as well as learning and behavioral disabilities. In Johnson's later essay, *Every Child Can Learn, Every Child Must Learn, Part II*, she recommends the following:

1. Let us develop an adapted version of the National Standard Curriculum in an effort to further accommodate our different learners. With such a step, it would further mean that the assessments at the local and national levels would mirror the curriculum our children are taught from. The curriculum should be designed in levels so that based on the child's current level of development, teachers are better able to facilitate them and assist them in their academic career.
2. The national examinations should reflect the student's cognitive level and the adapted curriculum. The student's assessment results would play a critical role in the way they are grouped for instruction and assessments.
3. It may be fruitful to conduct a nationwide research to ascertain the volume/number of our students with mild to moderate special needs, who have been able to go through our education system and are gainfully employed/making meaningful contributions to the society. Also, we should examine the percentage of students with special needs who get enrolled in and complete a Heart Trust

NSTA programme and can sustain themselves and contribute to the development of the society.
4. If the Ministry of Education is to be seen as a change agent in the field of education, it must take seriously its role in developing policies and programmes that will benefit all its constituents. Every child must learn, every child can learn must be more than a catchphrase. It must be demonstrated throughout the education system with the ministry taking the lead role. (Johnson, 2022b, para. 8–12)

Again, an adherence to the tenets of universal education are noble, but must include a consideration of how we provide differentiated learning opportunities in *all* schools and classrooms. Accountability and professional development measures focused on teachers require the provision of training and resources needed to adequately address these basic pedagogical issues. Additionally, teachers' voices must be a part of system-wide school reform. As it stands today, these issues make popular fodder for the newspapers but there is little forward movement where it counts; the Ministry and the schools.

Despite independence in 1962, educators still replicate a system of education that treats teachers as semi-professionals, at best, and perpetuates schools that are overcrowded and underresourced. The ironies are obvious, but overturning this system is seldom a part of any discussion. No one disagrees that there are problems, but the obstacles to change seem overwhelming. In a 2014 essay in *The Gleaner*, National Education Inspectorate Report: More Schools Failing, it was reported that, "With the 2014 National Education Inspectorate (NEI) report revealing that most primary and secondary schools were failing in their education delivery, Minister of Education Ronald Thwaites said immediate and drastic intervention would be made to improve performance" (Cunningham, 2014, para. 1). In conclusion, the essay acknowledged that, "This means we have sufficient evidence to show that the level of performance system-wide is mediocre, with the primary schools lagging behind the secondary ones" (Cunningham, para. 6). Recommendations for addressing these issues focused on the following, "Effective schools were defined by having strong leadership, a clear school mission, quality teaching and learning, a safe and orderly climate, transparent and effective monitoring of students' progress, and high expectations and parental involvement" (para. 9). As noted in the article, school leadership is key to school improvement, but noticeably absent from these recommendations is a consideration of the role of teachers acting in leadership roles to advocate and initiate meaningful and sustainable change.

In another essay, *Fix Our Broke and Broken Education System*, the writer states that "it is clear to us that Jamaica's education system fails to address the needs of our workforce" ("Fix Our Broke and Broken System," 2016, para. 2). Again, the focus is on the impact of drugs and crime and a misalignment of the education system to the needs of families and communities. In this particular article, the recommendations for fixing the system focused on social and economic issues. They propose reforms that would hopefully yield quick and substantial results:

- Remodel existing, under utilised schools and infrastructure to create special regional institutes that cater to the interests and competences of individual students for example high schools for: the visual and performing arts, more specialised institutions for physical education and sports, development and technologies, and entrepreneurship, agriculture, like the so far successful remodelling of Trench Town High School into a polytechnic college.
- Develop a streamlined process for the monitoring and assessment of overall progress of students through the development of personal learning plans (PLPs) and separate students based on areas of interest and regional location rather than the traditional versus non-traditional institutions that currently exist.
- Base classroom instructions on what was gathered in these PLPs and ensure there are various academic intervention programmes in these specialised schools. ("Fix Our Broke and Broken Education System," 2016, para. 20–25)

All good ideas; however, two questions are self-evident; first, "Where are the voices of teachers?" and second, "How do you implement these 'solutions' if there is no teacher involvement?" If how we define the problem determines the solution, a continuing focus on everything except teachers will continue to undermine and ultimately guarantee failure for even the most rudimentary efforts to solve educational problems.

Jamaican schools are not static institutions, but rather dynamic and fluid instruments of society. There is no one description of *all* teachers or *all* schools; they change. However, schools and schooling in Jamaica is a national endeavor, and as such, changes to schools, schooling, and the teaching profession must begin at a national level. Disrupting that narrative and creating challenges to the status quo are initiatives that require a vision and leadership. However, leadership is not necessarily a top–down process. The previously discussed idea of beginning with the "end in mind," is a concept that I use frequently in my work on revisioning education and schooling. I pulled the idea from Stephen Covey (2013) because I like the notion that we have to have a vision of where we want to go before we can begin to construct a road to that destination. And those familiar with my work will also recognize my fondness for provoking discussions that question taken-for-granted assumptions about how we do schools. George and Louise Spindler, educational anthropologists, used to "push" researchers to "make the familiar strange...and the strange familiar" (Spindler & Spindler, 1982, pp. 20–46). Jamaican education continues to mimic and replicate the British models that dominated the organization, process, and product of education at the time of independence. Changes and challenges to that model are slow to come; for many, the view is the system is not broken so why fix it. And yet, statistics indicate that the system is broken and that today, in the 21st century, it is more imperative than ever before that we address the needs of families and students attempting to navigate both the relevance of education both nationally and internationally. After reading this chapter, consider the following questions:

1. When considering the ideology of *all children can learn, all children must learn*, "What does that really mean for the organization of schools and resources?" Think about the implications of truly honoring this belief in all educational work in all communities. What would be required? What changes would need to be made to ensure that all children learn regardless of social class or disability?
2. Considering all the dimensions of curriculum; for example, purposes and aims, content of the curriculum, roles of teachers and students, and assessment, "How would these be realigned to reflect a focus on ensuring that *all children can learn, all children must learn?*"
3. How would professional development for all educational leaders be impacted by a renewed focus on the tenets of *all children can learn, all children must learn?*

3

Jamaican Teachers

Walk Good

Talking about Jamaican teachers is complicated by the knowledge that there is no one prototype of a Jamaican teacher. Each teacher has her or his own story that is defined by personal circumstances; history, demographics, experience, personality, and so on. Everyone's story is different. However, in this book the stories will overlap, and hopefully, common themes will resonate with those who work with teachers across the island. I am not alone in loving a good Jamaican story; the story below was shared on National Teachers' Day by a colleague of mine, Dr. Tom Oren, regarding his work with Jamaican teachers:

> Many years ago, I was walking around a vacant lot in New Kingston that would later become Emancipation Park. During that walk an older gentleman and I began having a nice conversation. Amongst other things we discussed, I said how much I admired his walking stick. As we went our separate ways the walking stick ended up in my hands, as a gift or through purchase, I don't recall. I bring this up because the walking stick is made of lignum vitae, which for me has always symbolized the unbreakable strength I see in

teachers in Jamaica. There are many attributes I admire in Jamaican educators: resilience, persistence, determination, patience, and respect. I've seen these in myriad ways in your interactions with me, your colleagues, and students. These have been constant throughout all the years I have known you. Because of who you are I have no doubt you can become one of the best educational systems in the world. The most important element in order to reach this standard is a system of TRUST. The trust that administrators, parents, community, and nation put in you that you are educating the nations' children to the highest standard. When administrators walk into your classroom it's not to put a tick on an evaluation form but to learn from what you are doing so they can pass that knowledge to other educators. When the ministry sends a team of individuals to a school or classroom it is not to evaluate or denigrate but rather to see how they can establish collaborative relationships within and between schools to share knowledge and foster shared responsibility. When parents send their child to school they know it will get the same quality education whether it is in rural St. Elizabeth, the intercity communities of Kingston or Montego Bay or the more affluent communities in Jamaica. Education is equitable throughout the nation rather than based upon where you live or what you can afford. How you build trust between all the entities to achieve these goals is your biggest challenge. You have given up so much to be where you are today. Realize how unique and special you are. Be humble in that knowledge. Let me leave you with a word you may or may not know: parrhesia. It is an ancient Greek word that has slightly different meaning if used as a noun or verb. As a noun, it means "one who speaks truth to power." My hope to each of you who continue this journey, find TRUST and PARRHESIA... Happy Teachers day... Walk Good. (Oren, 2021)

While I may not agree with Dr. Oren's positive assessment regarding the top-down collaboration between teachers and administrators or the presence of educational equity; there is too much data to the contrary, I do support his recognition of the strength and perseverance that exists among Jamaican teachers and throughout the Jamaican culture. I also present his story as evidence of varying perspectives regarding the strengths and weaknesses within the Jamaican education system; I am certain that my views may be seen as a bit harsh by some readers. Unfortunately, Jamaican teachers understand *walking good*. In Patois, *walking good* means to stay out of trouble or to be careful; an admonition that Jamaican teachers will heed if they want to keep their jobs and potentially "speak truth to power." Many of the Jamaican teachers I have encountered are not trusting that their efforts to seek empowerment and assert their voices will be welcomed by those in more powerful positions. As such, the subjects discussed in this chapter have to be carefully navigated.

Jamaican Teachers and Compensation

Teachers are leaving the island in record numbers. On February 14, 2020, Alphea Saunders wrote that 390 teachers had left the island in the past 5 months (Saunders, 2020). While this represented only 1.6% of the approximately 25,000 teachers, the annual effect of continued migration continues to build. In Saunders essay, Karl Samuda, the minister without portfolio who is overseeing the education ministry is quoted as saying, "The fact of the matter is that there are a number of opportunities that arise for our teachers to go abroad in search of more salaries and conditions of work, and it is undeniable that in some situations in some of our schools and the environment in which the teachers have to work, are not ideal" (para. 10). *Au Contraire* argues Winston Smith, the newly installed president of the Jamaican Teachers' Association. He warns that

> if negotiations for a better salary package are not accelerated, a resulting mass migration of teachers will dwarf the exodus of the Israelites out of Egypt in the biblical story. I am saying to all those who are hearing me, if this negotiation does not come through quickly, with the teachers in mind, Jamaica will see an exodus of teachers that will make the exodus in Moses' day look like child's play. We are calling on the minister of education [and] finance and the public service to avert that tragedy. Colleagues, it appears as if this scant regard is shown to the profession and as a result these countries are benfiting from our expertise, while our Jamaican students and the country suffer. (Hines, 2021, paras. 7–8)

Nevertheless, on March 10, 2022, Janet Silvera (2022), wrote an essay for *The Gleaner* suggesting that there was no mass exodus of teachers. She cites the following:

> Jamaica's Minister of Education Fayval Williams has dispelled the notion that there is a "mass exodus" of teachers from the classroom annually. While acknowledging that compensation of teachers was a sore point, Williams said that there was no empirical data giving credence to the narrative that educators were leaving the island in droves for better-paying markets. Williams disclosed that 731, or three per cent, of the country's 24,000 teachers left the profession between 2020 and 2021. That ratio, she argued, was within the range of internationally accepted benchmarks—whether in the education or other sectors. (paras. 1–3)

Two very different perspectives on the issue of teacher attrition are presented here; and yet, there can be no denying that the migration of Jamaican teachers has been a pervasive topic of discussion for many years. Jamaican teachers are well-educated and attractive to school districts in other countries seeking minority teachers to fill open positions in urban schools.

Taken as one set of data, the numbers do not seem alarming; however, the numbers continue to rise each year and questions about teachers' work and compensation continue to be cited as major reasons that teachers are dissatisfied with their jobs. On May 7, 2022, Winston Smith was again cited by Anthony Lewis in *The Gleaner*. In the article titled, "JTA Head Again Blasts Gov't Over Low Wages," he passionately argued,

> One of the most striking things is that persons who have absolutely no idea what it means to be a teacher seem to be the ones who are leading the argument about what ought to be done and what should not be done, he said. I believe that it is time, as educators, we rise up and stand in our rightful position and declare that as long as we are the vanguard of this noble profession, this institution that continues to give even when others are taking, we defend and protect every ounce of what we have and what we are seeking to do. (Lewis, 2022, paras. 6–8)

These challenges strike to the core of the teaching profession and highlight the "scrappiness" of the ongoing debates about the value of teachers and their importance to any serious efforts to improve the schools. Information from this same essay indicates that "in February, approximately 68 per cent of the JTA's membership voted to accept the Government's four per cent wage offer. As part of the deal, teachers will receive a book and software allowance of $40,000 per year" (Lewis, 2022, para. 12). These numbers indicate the willingness of a relatively small group of teachers to accept whatever is offered with only limited argument and debate. The fear expressed by some is that if the offer was not accepted; the next offer (if it comes) may be worse. The agency and power of teachers to negotiate for both reasonable compensation and better working conditions are negligible. When valuable resources, like teachers, are squandered, the offended have three choices; shut up and give up, find another job, or simply leave. *Walk good* my comrades.

> As recently as September, 2022, Education Minister, Fayval Williams, announced a 50% jump in teacher resignations since July (248 teachers). Once again, she was accused of downplaying the issue of teacher migration (Wilks, 2022, paras. 9–11)

Salaries and teacher attrition are serious issues that will continue to afflict Jamaican schools and defy efforts for school reform until fundamental problems associated with compensation and teacher working conditions are addressed by the Ministry.

Teacher Moonlighting in Jamaica

In 2018, I endeavored to better understand Jamaican teachers' work by expanding my research on teacher moonlighting to consider the impact of this phenomenon on Jamaican teachers. In the United States, statistics dating back to the 1950s have consistently shown that at least 2/3 of all teachers moonlight (Blair, 2018a; Parham & Gordon, 2011). While there is no published research on teacher moonlighting among Jamaicans, it seemed likely that the phenomenon was also a part of the lives and work of Jamaican teachers. Earlier work on teachers moonlighting (Blair, 2018a) showed that the activity was deeply engrained in the lives and work of American teachers. Specifically, the research documented the following:

> Many teachers moonlight on a continual basis throughout their careers. Others moonlight according to needs, both personal and financial. In the past, numbers have varied because of inconsistencies in what is defined as moonlighting. Is moonlighting the work that teachers do in the summer or does it also include additional work during the school year? Additionally, when teachers assume extra responsibilities during the school year and receive stipends, should that also be considered moonlighting? When teachers were asked what constituted moonlighting behavior, all of the above could be included. In her research, teachers suggested that additional compensation for anything beyond their contractual teaching responsibilities should be considered teacher moonlighting. (Blair, 2018a, p. 1)

Teacher moonlighting has regularly been documented as a pervasive part of the fabric of teachers' work; a dimension of teaching that is well-known, but seldom mentioned in discussions of the teaching profession. It seemed likely that with the concerns regularly expressed by Jamaican teachers about salary and working conditions, teacher moonlighting would also be prevalent in Jamaica.

Teacher moonlighting in Jamaica is, indeed, a phenomenon, and while the numbers are different from those in the United States, they, nevertheless, reveal a pattern of behavior endemic to teachers' work globally. Two hundred ninety-nine (299) teachers across the island participated in a study of moonlighting among Jamaican teachers. It should be noted that a sample of only 299 teachers is small and represents approximately one percent of the nearly 25,000 teachers across the island. However, despite the small sample size, the participants in this study do demonstrate the presence of teacher moonlighting in Jamaica. The findings revealed that 111 teachers (37%) had additional sources of income to supplement their teaching salaries; 188 teachers (63%) did not participate in moonlighting activities. Among the moonlighters, 44 (23%) were males and 148 (77%)

were females. The average reported salaries of these teachers were between $5,000–$10,000 USD. The moonlighting jobs varied; for example, taxi driving, chicken farming, dance instruction, tutoring, retail, and so on. However, overwhelmingly, the primary reason given for moonlighting was financial; teachers strongly felt that their teaching salaries were not sufficient to cover basic expenses. Reasons for moonlighting were the following:

- to be better able to take care of my objectives
- self-gentrification
- opportunity fell into my lap
- moonlighting to enhance my skills
- to gain extra income for family
- current salary is insufficient
- salary cannot support my life
- the need for additional income
- to help out at dance school which is my alma mater
- to gain the experience
- income from teaching not enough to sustain family
- to learn a new skill and to increase my income
- need additional income and professional development
- passion
- house and car payments
- to further assist in paying tuition and overhead costs
- I started this business because the salary is very low
- to earn extra cash for WCU tuition

These findings are consistent with previous studies of teacher moonlighting in the United States. While most teachers indicated that they moonlight for additional income, it is interesting that for many of them the moonlighting jobs complement their work as teachers or satisfy needs (both personal and professional) that are not being met by teaching alone (Blair, 2018a). Perhaps, more concerning; however, is that among the teachers who participated in this study, a large number of teachers indicated a desire to leave the profession. Among the 299 teachers who participated in this research, 35% indicated a desire to leave teaching—47 out of 111 moonlighters (42%) and 56 out of 188 non-moonlighters (30%) indicated that they plan to leave teaching. The reasons given varied;

- the indiscipline of students and parents, limited room for advancing myself financially;
- poor attitude, low salary, lack of teaching materials;
- need to do self-care and explore other avenues;

- to start my own business;
- I think I have outgrown this stage and I would like to explore another level;
- the tasks have become overwhelming;
- I have become weary of the system;
- the demands for the job are getting greater; paperwork, culture of students, salary;
- job too demanding;
- due to the low wages being offered us;
- too stressful;
- high stress and low pay;
- the salary is unsatisfactory; my safety is at-risk;
- working hours, stress level, salary, and so on;
- the work level, constant behavioral problems of students, lack of parental support, and a lot more;
- underpayment, depression;
- excessive administrative duties and lack of appreciation; and
- it's too demanding on the body and mind.

Issues with salary, behavior, stress and excessive work demands were consistently expressed by those wanting to leave the profession. There are myriad ways to interpret and understand teacher moonlighting, but Stuart Hall's (1980) theory of preferred, negotiated and oppositional ways of *reading* as part of a public pedagogical exploration of social contexts and popular media is useful in this context. Hall (a Jamaican-British academic) articulated his ideas about "encoding/decoding" cultural texts, for example, newspapers, movies, television, social media images, and so on, and described his theory as having three components. First, one can view teachers' work using the tools of oppositional reading, in this case, teaching is inherently a political act where key political actors (educational leaders) are concerned with gaining the submission of teachers... a predominantly female profession... to the larger causes of capitalist interests that want to define teaching and learning as inputs and outputs that can be carefully measured and controlled, e.g., accountability efforts. Teachers' pay and teachers' lack of voice, autonomy, and respect are mechanisms for securing their allegiance, and thus, maintaining control in an institution that does not consider their needs nor those of their students as primary. Calls for higher teacher salaries are admirable, but stop short of demanding a complete overhaul of a system that ignores the larger issues associated with teachers' work and perpetuates a system where teachers need to plead, beg, or even threaten to strike in order to be recognized as deserving the full professional status of other comparable professions, and thus, paid appropriate wages. Teacher moonlighting can be seen as a way for teachers to negotiate a survival strategy in lieu of substantive changes to the profession. At least with teacher moonlighting, teachers have a modicum of control over their work lives and the income they are able to generate.

Second, the lack of voice, status, autonomy, and/or respect inherent to the teaching profession mirrors the challenges faced by women across society. In many ways, the teacher moonlighting stories highlighted in the news perpetuate an image of teachers as victims of their own poor career choices. While teacher moonlighting reflects the independent actions of teachers attempting to address the deficiencies of teachers' work, teachers are portrayed as merely *reacting* to low salaries but not as *activists* questioning the sources of their oppression and the political ideologies served by keeping teachers at a semi-professional status.

And third, the *silences* regarding teacher moonlighting and what it says about teachers and the culture of teaching are deafening. Most references to teacher moonlighting simply lament the challenges of teaching in schools where the salaries are inadequate, seriously inadequate in many cases. And yet, these discussions ignore the fact that teachers are better educated than most of the politicians making decisions about the teaching profession. Experience and education would seem to demand teachers have a front row seat in policy decision-making, and yet, teachers seldom participate in educational decision-making. And frequently, when teachers do complain, they are bullied in the media and treated as petulant children.

While teacher moonlighting is seldom acknowledged or discussed by teachers and administrators; in Jamaica, it seems to be commonly accepted that teachers have other jobs in addition to teaching. If anything, teacher moonlighting in Jamaica is seen as commendable and indicative of the work ethic of teachers. Teachers who are portrayed in movies and on television often see their second jobs incorporated into the story as common behavior and not worthy of note. Silence regarding the issue of teacher moonlighting is not the problem; the problem is that despite mandates for higher levels of teacher preparation and the addition of new roles and responsibilities to teachers' work, we continue to ignore the many contradictory facets of teacher preparation, teachers' work, and the challenges faced by individuals doing some of the most important jobs in society. If we define teacher moonlighting as simply a problem associated with teacher pay, we ignore the larger realities of the problems inherent to teachers' work; for example, status, power, autonomy, lack of leadership opportunities, and learned helplessness.

Studies of teacher moonlighting have previously demonstrated that moonlighting has both positive and negative outcomes for teachers' work

(Blair, 2018a). In one sense, teacher moonlighting addresses the dissatisfaction that teachers feel because of insufficient salaries; however, in another sense, the difficult and challenging conditions of teachers' work are not assuaged, and if anything, the dissatisfaction continues to grow. Knowing both the strengths and weaknesses of teacher moonlighting, I still contend that the time and energy of teachers could be better utilized if their work was school-related and focused on solving the most intransigent educational problems. While much of my research on teacher moonlighting has focused on teachers in the United States, the findings are, nevertheless, applicable to Jamaican teachers. The following summarizes the relationship between teacher moonlighting and school reform efforts and is relevant to Jamaican teachers:

> School reform affects everyone involved in the work that takes place in schools and classrooms, and yet too often we focus on the wrong problems, and subsequently, the wrong solutions. Increasing teachers' salaries will not stop teacher moonlighting and it will not produce happy teachers. Lasting changes in the teaching profession should emphasize improved working conditions and recognition of problems inherent in the "doing" of a teacher's job. Moonlighting has implications for reform in the area of teachers' work. This topic has long been ignored by those making decisions about the future of public education, but the phenomenon has not been ignored by textbook authors or by the many teachers who participate in moonlighting activities. In the present forum of debate and discussion about educational issues, a reconsideration of teacher moonlighting seems timely and appropriate. It is possible that a better understanding of the phenomenon may lead to a consideration of the important ways that we could change the nature and structure of teachers' work, and, most importantly, a consideration of the need for a strong profession with a level of training and responsibility that would yield higher compensation. The difficulty of attaining this goal is obvious; however, if we embrace the idea that how we define the problem determines the solution, then a vision for the reform of teaching that focuses on issues related to the professional status of teachers will ultimately produce outcomes that are preferable to our current condition. The growth of a stronger teaching profession would be facilitated by a recognition of the problems that afflict all teachers, moonlighting and non-moonlighting. (Blair, 2018a, pp. 228–229)

It is concerning that a third of the 299 teachers in this study want to leave teaching. This is a serious reminder that all is not well with teachers in Jamaica. It can also be argued that the teachers who participated in this study are graduate students, and as such, represent some of the most highly skilled and motivated teachers in the profession. If Jamaica loses these teachers to other jobs or even teacher placements overseas, the loss to the country is irreparable.

Teachers' Work and the Voices of Teachers

Individuals entered the teaching profession in Jamaica aware of the challenges associated with becoming a teacher; many entered the profession hoping to make a difference in the lives of others. The journey to become a teacher in Jamaica is not significantly different from what happens in other countries. Teachers are often inspired by their own teachers or family members who are teachers. In many cases, it is the encouragement of others that leads to the decision to become a teacher. I never fail to be struck by the compassion and enthusiasm I encounter among the teachers I encounter on the island. While their personal journeys to the teaching profession may vary, they persevere with commitment and passion. Teachers in my leadership study discussed this journey in response to the questions: Describe yourself as a teacher. How did you get here? Background? Education? Job Experiences?

> I always wanted to be a teacher. My sixth-grade teacher was an awesome teacher and I decided from 11 years old that I want to be a teacher. I want to make a difference in childrens' lives. I have a teaching diploma from St. Joseph's Teachers College and a Bachelor of Science in education from Western Carolina University. (JM2-22)

> There were many hurdles and challenges that I came across to get to the point of being here as a teacher. I was born and raised in a small extended family inclusive of grandmother, parents, sisters and brother, in a nearby community to the main town Mandeville. Growing up, life was a challenge especially financially, but dependency on the lord saw us through. I garnered my kindergarten education right within my community for a school founded by members of a church. Today I proudly appreciate the foundation that was instilled within and seek to promote their continued efforts in giving students a solid foundation to education. (JM1-22)

> In my final two years at the Vere Technical high school, located in Hayes Clarendon. I had a very influential teacher who really showed interest in my overall development as a student and I admired him for that. As a result I decided that I wanted to make a positive impression on other students in the same way that he did to me. After leaving high school I worked as a pre-trained at a basic school where I was a teacher's aide; you really have to love children to work in basic school. It was a challenge for the month, it begins to grow on you. I worked there for year, then I went into BPO industry for two years and then I got into the G.C. Foster College of Physical Education and Sport. (JM14-21)

I am where I am today because of my grandmother and my mom's prayers firstly, also the experience I got as a child in the role of leadership. Becoming a teacher was only natural, I went through other employment institutions however they were just not fulfilling, I am complete when I teach, I feel like I am helping someone's life if it is even just to learn to write or spell their name I feel like I have made a meaningful impact on someone lives. (JM16-19)

My only job experience is the school where I started my first teaching job I am still employed there. I stay there because I am very comfortable due to my working environment. (JM18-21)

My job experience is very rich as I have taught at different types of Institutions and at various levels. I started at the primary level Carmel Primary where I learned to deal with small children. I have also taught at a co-ed institution at the McGrath High School, as well as an all-girl school, St. Andrew High School for Girls. I also experienced working at a shift school, at the Old Harbour High school. I have worked with female and male principals and a variety of teacher leaders with combinations of different teaching and leadership styles, all of which have contributed to my growth and development as a teacher leader. I have adopted the good habits and emulated the best practices. (JM17-19)

In the teacher leadership research study, teachers regularly expressed their commitment and passion for being a teacher. In Jamaica, much like the United States, teaching has always been a career path for working-class women who come from less advantaged backgrounds and saw their female teachers (or family members who were teachers) as female role models making a difference in childrens' lives through the student–teacher relationship. The path to becoming a teacher provided access to greater educational opportunities and led to a career that offered some small level of authority and a paycheck. And sometimes, these female teachers saw themselves as activists empowering future generations of young girls to mentor and advocate on behalf of other children desperately in need of guidance (Weiler, 1988). These role models inspired and motivated their female students to follow in their footsteps and continue the tradition of becoming teachers. The students in the teacher leadership study regularly discussed the trajectory to becoming a teacher, and while many of them expressed dissatisfaction with working conditions and compensation, most remained very committed to the work; teaching satisfies a basic need to contribute to society and help others.

In 2004, the Task Force on Educational Reform—Jamaica—A Transformed Education System recommended, "All teachers to complete Bachelor's Degree in Education. Holders of degrees in other subject disciplines must complete a diploma in Teacher Education" (Task Force on Educational

Reform Final Report, 2004, p. 94). In 2010, Williams and Staulters (2010) described the training and credentials of teachers in Jamaican schools:

> There are two routes to teacher preparation in Jamaica: Educators are either initially trained at the teacher preparation college level or the university level. There are several teacher preparation colleges in Jamaica, which provide three years of instruction beyond high school to future educators. Graduates of these programs earn a Diploma in Education, which allows them to teach at the primary through secondary levels of education.... Regardless of teaching improvement policies, many educators in Jamaica, especially in the rural communities, continue to be trained at the teacher college level. (p. 99)

In the past, many teachers who were interested in advancing their credentials chose to attend universities where they could earn a Bachelor's Degree or even a Master's in education. More recently, the Ministry of Education and Youth (MOEY) has sanctioned mandates requiring that all teachers be licensed at the Bachelor's level. The Jamaica Teaching Council Bill (2022) re-ignited the controversy,

> Recently, in Parliament, the Jamaica Teachers' Association was invited to air its concerns about the Bill. Its president, Winston Smith, shared his discomfort with the definition used to characterise a teacher, noting that it would automatically exclude certain specialists as well as teachers who only have a diploma or a certificate. In terms of qualifications, the Bill proposes that a teacher is anyone with a bachelor of education or a first degree with a postgraduate diploma in teaching. (Madden, 2022, para. 8)

The focus on advancing the education of teachers at all levels was an important part of the Task Force on Educational Reform—Jamaica—A Transformed Education System (2004). The impact of these recommendations was a dramatic increase in the number of teachers seeking a bachelor's degree in education through various tertiary institutions across the island. Additionally, the advanced training of teachers included a renewed interest in providing equitable opportunities to students needing special services; special education programs of studies are in high demand and a new population of special education teachers has emerged to meet the needs of children with disabilities. The Development of Education, National Report of Jamaica by the Planning and Development Division, Ministry of Education (2008), was published 4 years later and it affirmed that the Jamaican education system continued to face many challenges in the 21st century (p. 2); however, most of the challenges mirrored the ones described in the Taskforce on Educational Reform Final Report (2004). The report (2008) discusses teacher quality and focuses its recommendations around educational attainment and professional development. In the report, they document that only 65% of Jamaican teachers are college graduates (p. 11). Regarding leadership work, they recommend a group be appointed to work on leadership, performance management, school improvement planning, and special education (Planning and Development Division, 2008, p. 4). Previously noted concerns about the preparation and overall quality of teachers is discussed and plans for supporting advanced academic studies as well as professional development are noted (pp. 19–20). Again, it is striking that neither the Task Force on Educational Reform—Jamaica—A Transformed Education System (2004) nor the Development of Education, National Report of Jamaica (2008) mention consultation with teachers or the inclusion of teacher voices in the determination of the problems or a consideration of potential solutions; teachers are talked about but seldom get a "seat at the table" in discussions about school reform that include a critique of the quality and content of teacher expertise and knowledge.

More recently, the Jamaica Teacher Council (JTC) Bill (2022) has generated renewed interest, discussion, and yes, controversy regarding the professionalization of teaching in Jamaica. The JTC was originally established in response to the Task Force on Educational Reform Report (2004). The JTC Bill, 2022, furthers the work of the JTC and highlights a perceived need "to regulate entry into the teaching profession and to develop and monitor the professional standards of teacher competence and practice" (University of West Indies, para. 2). The Ministry of Education and Youth (MOEY) endorsed the JTC and gave it responsibility for the following: (a) regulating the teaching profession, (b) building and maintaining competences of teachers, and (c) raising the public profile of the profession as a change agent to societal reform and development in the context of the Social Policy vision for Jamaica (Jamaica Teaching Council, 2022, para. 3). The JTC acknowledges that there is "evidence of global acceptance that education for all will not be a reality until the challenges of teachers and teaching are met" (para. 7). The response to the continuing debate about the JTC highlights the fundamental issues that plague the profession in 2022. President of the Teachers' Colleges of Jamaica Dr. Garth Anderson addresses the problems with the JTC in the following:

> There is no need to police the teachers; instead, what is needed is to further professionalise the profession. He expressed that, though he supports the intent of the Bill, which is to set standards and guide the profession, many teachers feel that the Bill primarily seeks to criminalise teachers.
>
> Teachers often feel that they cannot catch a break. They are in the spotlight all year round and have to deal with unruly students, overcrowded classes, limited resources, inadequate compensation, and difficult administrators.

> Understandably, adding this Bill to their daily 'miseries' will only make their job more burdensome. Nonetheless, it is important to have oversight of the profession. (Maddin, 2022, paras. 4–5)

Thus, after two decades of debate, the role of the JTC is still questionable. An emphasis on teacher competency and accountability is the focus of its mandates while ignoring the prerequisite need for the involvement of teachers' voices in defining a process that promotes the professional status of teachers and recognizes teacher knowledge and expertise.

Many previous texts have described Jamaican schools but only a few have highlighted the important roles played by the teachers who work in these schools (Bissessar, 2017; Blair & Williams, 2021; Evans, 2001; Miller, 2013). In fact, it is startling to read numerous books on Jamaican schools and education and see a broad focus on "leadership" without seeing a discussion of elevating teachers to leadership roles (Heremuru, 2013). While I understand that there are many aspects of Jamaican schools that I may not understand or have firsthand knowledge about; for example, curriculum reform, finance, Ministry politics and procedures, the focus of my work has been on understanding teachers' lives and work while trying to help them negotiate a path towards the promotion of teacher leadership as a way to gain higher professional status and simultaneously improve the schools; for example, school culture, teacher retention, higher achievement. Evans (2001) in her notable work, *Inside Jamaican Schools*, described the following scenario in Jamaica,

> When teachers are mentioned in the public discourse on education, their shortcomings are often highlighted. Criticism of teachers stems from our high expectations for schools as well as from the memory of our own teachers. Many of us have an idealized image of our former teachers; the behavior, conduct, and performance of contemporary teachers fall short of what we can recall of our own teachers. The fact that teaching appears easy, and does not appear to require any special knowledge, partly explains such criticism. (p. 31)

Seeing teachers as lacking skills and knowledge contributes to the lack of professional status and the tendency to blame them for problems in the schools. Repeatedly, task forces and national reports highlight potential solutions to Jamaica's educational problems; and yet, none of these solutions acknowledge the powerful resource that Jamaican teachers represent. As previously stated, teachers in Jamaica are better educated than ever before in their history; teachers are ready to take leadership positions and guide the transformation of 21st century Jamaican schools, and yet, the significance of their contributions, and the role that teacher leadership could play in the progress of education is seldom acknowledged in school reform efforts. Carmel Roofe (2020) discussed the characteristics of teachers who participated in her 2019 study of teacher leadership. She described the ZRESS in teacher leaders character as, zealous, resilient, eager, self-evaluative, and solutions oriented (pp. 107–108). These teachers were "led by a core set of values and principles that guided their actions as they sought to achieve cognitive, emotional and social justice for all" (p. 108). In conclusion, Roofe found that "having these teachers in any school should be the catalyst for ongoing profession development, especially when new reforms are implemented in schools" (p. 108). Far too often, teachers are political pawns in much larger battles to keep the control of schools and teachers' work in the hands of the few who have the political capital and power to continue making decisions that *do not* promote the work of teachers, but rather denigrates their efforts and relegates them to subordinate positions. In this book, the voices of Jamaican teachers are part of the effort to recognize their work and suggest that teacher leadership is the only viable road to school reform and improvement. There may be few answers in this book; however, if this text can serve as a foundation for critical discussions around key questions about the restructuring of schools and promotion of teachers to full professional status then it will have served its purpose.

In the Jamaican Education Transformation Commission (2022), The Reform of Education in Jamaica 2021—The Report references are made to the deficiencies in the pedagogical training of teachers and the need for "incentivization and the enhanced professionalization of teaching" (p. 33), there is still no discussion of making teachers' voices or even teacher leadership a serious part of school reform. Rather, the focus is on increased accountability, professional development and training; all good things if presented within a larger vision of a teaching profession that prepares a roadmap of a profession that includes leadership capacity building that includes all major stakeholders in the process of defining what accountability looks like and the content of professional development and training. As long as there is a patriarchal attitude towards teachers that places them in a subordinate role as individuals to be *talked about* rather than equal participants in the conversation, meaningful changes will not occur. I am reminded of Paulo Freire's (2000) discussion of the teacher–student relationship and the banking concept of education and how it relates to the role of teachers in a decolonized country:

> In the banking concept of education, knowledge is a gift bestowed by those who consider themselves knowledgeable upon those whom they consider to know nothing. Projecting an absolute ignorance onto others, a characteristic of the ideology of oppression, negates education and knowledge as processes of inquiry. The teacher presents himself to his students as their necessary opposite; by considering their ignorance absolute, he justifies his

own existence. The students, alienated like the slave in the Hegelian dialectic, accept their ignorance as justifying the teachers existence—but unlike the slave, they never discover that they educate the teacher.

This solution is not (nor can it be) found in the banking concept. On the contrary, banking education maintains and even stimulates the contradiction through the following attitudes and practices, which mirror oppressive society as a whole:

   a. the teacher teaches and the students are taught;
   b. the teacher knows everything and the students know nothing;
   c. the teacher thinks and the students are thought about;
   d. the teacher talks and the students listen—meekly;
   e. the teacher disciplines and the students are disciplined;
   f. the teacher chooses and enforces his choice, and the students comply;
   g. the teacher acts and the students have the illusion of acting through the action of the teacher;
   h. the teacher chooses the program content, and the students (who were not consulted) adapt to it;
   i. the teacher confuses the authority of knowledge with his or her own professional authority, which she and he sets in opposition to the freedom of the students;
   j. the teacher is the Subject of the learning process, while the pupils are mere objects. (pp. 72–73)

In many ways, the relationship between Jamaican teachers and the "educational leaders" in Jamaica mirror this dichotomy and highlights how the ideology of oppression functions to keep teachers powerless and subject to the whims of those in authority positions.

   1. educational leaders dictate curriculum, policy, and products of education and the teachers implement the curriculum, policy, and products that they are given;
   2. educational leaders know everything and the teachers seem to know minimal content; they do not have access to prerequisite skills and knowledge needed to be decision-makers;
   3. educational leaders think and the teachers are thought about;
   4. educational leaders talk and the teachers listen;
   5. educational leaders discipline and demand accountability and the teachers have little input into neither the details of what the accountability will look like nor how those "falling short" will be managed;
   6. educational leaders choose and enforce policies and procedures, and the teachers comply;
   7. educational leaders act and the teachers have the illusion of acting through their actions as teachers;

8. educational leaders choose the program content, and the teachers (who were not consulted) adapt to it;
9. educational leaders confuse the authority of knowledge with his or her own professional authority, which she and he sets in opposition to the freedom of the teachers to act on their personal pedagogical knowledge; and
10. educational leaders determine the form and content of the learning process, while the teachers comply with the directions of those in positions of authority.

If one accepts... or at least, entertains... this proposition, it is easy to see how the current system in Jamaica does nothing to nurture the critical consciousness and creativity of teachers, but rather, reinforces passive acceptance of the status quo and renders teachers powerless to negotiate changes in teaching, learning and the training of teachers. In a similar vein, Hyacinth Evans (2001) noted the following:

> We all have, to some varying degrees, internalized the messages of a postcolonial society. Teachers are no exception. To change the practices which perpetuate inequality, lack of self-confidence and poor self-esteem on the part of students, requires a rethinking of the goal of education and a new role for the educator. (p. 148)

The reconciliation of these roles and an understanding of the powerful role of oppression must be a part of elevating the schools and the teaching profession to a higher level. We have to name the enemy of emancipatory education in order to begin to visualize the ways in which we can collaboratively fight against oppressive relationships that create obstacles to growth and transformation.

Jamaican teachers represent an incredibly valuable resource in Jamaica that has been largely ignored and treated as insignificant and perhaps even disposable. Jamaica has allowed and even encouraged other nations to recruit teachers from their ranks and school reform efforts seldom include the allocation of resources to upgrade and reward current teachers. In 2001, New York City public schools recruited teachers from Jamaica, Bahama, Trinidad, Grenada, St. Lucia, and the Dominican Republic. The teachers who applied to come to the United States were described in the following: "They were the cream of the crop" (King, 2001, para. 7). The average experience of the teachers was 20 years and while they had initially planned to recruit approximately 50 teachers, over 1,000 showed up across the islands. However, in 2011, the "experiment" was considered a failure by many of the teachers, "Thousands of Caribbean teachers who were lured to the United States with promises of better-paying jobs, improved educational opportunities, housing assistance, and the path to permanent residency are crying foul, claiming that they are victims of victimization" (King, 2001, para. 1). Silvera's (2011) exposé in *The Gleaner*, once again noted that teachers who are well-educated and skilled have been discarded and treated as something less than professionals. Particularly sad in this case is the fact that these teachers who were incredibly vulnerable to exploitation placed their trust in the promises of individuals from a first world country that offered opportunities that were not available in the Caribbean. Again, I am troubled by the fates of teachers who put their souls into work that is greeted with disdain by both their native countries, and too often, the countries that appealed to them with promises of riches and opportunities that never materialized. These teachers deserve respect and a nurturing of talent and gifts, but for most, that is an elusive dream and "settling" for whatever is offered becomes an uncomfortable reality.

This book presents a picture of 21st century Jamaican teachers; a picture that is informed by their voices, needs, and desires, but marred by the lack of status and respect granted to teachers. Using a model that I first encountered in Katzenmeyer and Moller (2009), I want to describe three aspects of the work lives of Jamaican teachers: "*Who* are Jamaican teachers?"; "*Where* do Jamaican teachers work?"; and "*How* do Jamaican teachers initiate meaningful, sustainable change in their professional lives and work in schools and classrooms?" (pp. 58–61). In order to understand the identity of Jamaican teachers, it is necessary to first consider a brief history of the profession. Hamilton (1997) provides an overview of the origins of the Jamaican teacher in a decolonized Jamaica:

> The post-emancipation formation of an educational system led to the obvious need for teachers and to the recognition that primary school teachers must be trained locally, since the supply of foreign missionaries and British-trained "imports" could not possibly keep up with demand. It appears that most "homegrown" teachers in the early years after emancipation gained access to the profession through a kind of apprenticeship system in which they served as "pupil-teachers" or "monitors" in local schools. This seems to have grown out of the missionaries' practice of singling out promising young men and training them as class leaders and lay preachers (cf. Sherlock & Bennett, 1998). In 1836 the Mico Charity established the Mico Institute (now Mico College) "for the benefit of African slaves made free and engaged in the work [of teaching]" (Sherlock & Bennett, 1998). The Institute was coeducational when it opened but soon accepted only men. Initially, most teachers were male, but by 1900 three teachers' colleges for women had opened (Bethabara Training College in 1861, Shortwood Training College in 1885, and St. Joseph's in 1897), and the proportion of women in the profession had risen to nearly half. By the 1960s the percentage of women

in the profession had risen to roughly 75%. (Hamilton, 1997, as cited in "Jamaica: Teaching Profession," n.d., para. 1)

Other problems discussed are the need to increase the number of certified teachers, retention and attrition issues, low salaries, and the lack of male teachers ("Jamaica: Teaching Profession," n.d., para. 2–3). It could be argued that the lack of adequate compensation for teachers contributes to all of the other issues. A profession dogged by paltry wages and limited status does not attract and retain the best and the brightest young people, male or female.

As a regular visitor and teacher on the island for over 30 years, I have conducted research with teachers where I have attempted to examine the status of the profession by looking at teacher leadership and teacher moonlighting. I have interviewed teachers, visited schools, and collected survey data that provides a "picture" of 21st century Jamaican teachers. This book presents Jamaican teachers as the unsung heroes of any story told about Jamaican schools and education. In fact, the importance of education is sacrosanct in Jamaica, and as such, Jamaican teachers are key players in Jamaica's struggles to overcome the low pay and even lower status of teachers as they persevere and attempt to guide and potentially empower a population of students who have even less power and status than the teachers.

Historically, Jamaican teachers have always experienced low pay and lack of status; however, they continued to show up and advocate for the children. While urban teachers will often have somewhat better physical conditions for teaching, rural teachers suffer under conditions that can only be described as reflecting a total disregard for the needs of poor, rural children. Again, this book tells a story; a story that is long and complicated and filled with the hills and valleys of an ongoing struggle that will ultimately define the progress of the country and the well-being and success of its citizens in twenty-first century Jamaica. Attempts by Jamaica to find its place in a global community will be hampered if the country and its leaders cannot figure out a way to successfully guide school reform that focuses on the recruitment and retention of good teachers, establishment of excellent schools and the promotion of school improvement in *all* schools, both urban and rural..

While Jamaican teachers frequently describe leadership scenarios that reflect the traditional norms of an autocratic leader who makes the decisions and teachers who follow their mandated roles and responsibilities, I am also encountering more schools where the principals are experimenting with building leadership capacity and transforming the school culture to meet the changing needs of 21st century schools and communities. As previously stated, there is no single example that characterizes all Jamaican schools, teachers or leaders. There are both incredibly good schools in Jamaica that are led by enthusiastic and brilliant teachers and leaders and there are schools still struggling to find the resources and support to build schools in a new image. Struggling under-resourced and overcrowded schools are frequently inhabited by teachers who sense the lack of value attached to the work they are doing. In many schools, teachers demonstrate their lack of motivation and commitment through chronic absenteeism and lateness; problems seen across Jamaica (Brown, 2013). Hill-Berry (2017) found that professionalism (or lack thereof) among Jamaican teachers included a variety of factors:

> Other factors that participants stated can be used to determine if colleagues are unprofessional include poor communication and interactions with peers, students and others; being disrespectful; having serious punctuality and time management issues; and when they are displaying no interest in personal and professional development. Other less popular responses provided by participants were educators' lacking commitment to the profession, disobeying the laws of the land, having issues associated with absenteeism, crossing boundaries in their relationships, and demonstrating incompetence. According to participants, they can also determine if a colleague is unprofessional by observing educators' actions and relationships especially those relationships with their professional body and with other professionals. (p. 37)

With regard to the overall professionalism of Jamaican teachers, a recent study by Hill-Berry (2017) found the following:

> A general view of whether Jamaican teachers are professional is still undecided. However, regardless of participants' wavering perceptions concerning the subject, their practices should be aligned with established principles as outlined by the JTA and the MOE. This alignment is essential since optimum levels of professionalism must be displayed among Jamaican educators as this has implications for their personal and professional development, and the growth and development of others with whom they interact.... Despite the fact that the Ministry of Education is assiduously working with the Jamaica Teachers' Association to amplify the levels of professionalism among educators, there is more to be done to get teachers to uphold professional standards, familiarize teachers with the JTA's code of ethics and to improve the levels of compliance with these professional codes and standards. In the meantime, educators should be encouraged to continuously seek and engage in professional development activities to augment their personal and professional growth; as well as the growth and development of others. The author therefore challenges educational leaders to hold educators to a higher level of excellence to ensure that they not only speak, but act professional, in order to promote adherence to their professional code of conduct and to professionalize the teaching profession. (pp. 40–41)

A need for professionalism among teachers cannot be disputed; however, I cannot help but feel a need to highlight that once again, teachers are talked about and not actively involved in defining teacher professionalism in 21st century schools. The Ministry of Education and Youth (MOEY) as well as the Jamaica Teachers Association are key actors in defining both policy and procedure, and are charged with the responsibility of holding teachers accountable. Does it seem unreasonable to attempt to align the concerns that teachers have about teachers' work and the dissatisfactions that accompany those concerns with the criteria for professional status? The reality is that as a group they are generally treated as semi-professionals that are somehow undeserving of the respect and autonomy that is granted most other professionals. Etzioni (1969) and (Lortie, 1969, 1975) were the first to identify teachers as semi-professionals that lacked even the most rudimentary characteristics of a real profession. While most would agree that teaching is a complicated intellectual task that requires problem solving around many pedagogical issues, teaching lacks control over credentials, professional development, specialization, authority, and compensation (Ingersoll & Merrill, 2011). If we want teachers to be professional, it would only seem reasonable to treat them as professionals as a starting place; however, efforts to provide teachers with control, autonomy, authority and adequate compensation are missing from most discussions of professionalism and professional development in Jamaica. Thinking about the ideas presented in this chapter, consider the following questions:

1. How do the professional qualifications of teachers align with expectations for professionals in other comparable fields? Think about compensation, credentials, regulation and licensing, autonomy, decision-making, authority, and so on.
2. Is teacher moonlighting a problem? Why or why not? What does teacher moonlighting among Jamaican teachers tell us about the current status and future of teachers' work?
3. Would mediated entry into the profession provide a reasonable option for recognizing and rewarding teachers according to educational credentials, skills and expertise, and educational outcomes?
4. What are the obstacles to teachers gaining full professional status? How they be overcome?
5. Is there a place in the public discourse on education for teachers' voices?

4

Jamaican Teachers and Schools

21st Century Teacher Leadership

When the best leader's work is done, the people say, "We did it ourselves."
—Lau Tzu

Judith Warren Little (1988) poignantly argued, "It is increasingly implausible that we could improve the performance of schools...without promoting leadership in teaching by teachers. She made this declaration almost 35 years ago, and yet, while her words ring true, the content, process, and product of teachers' work has not changed in the United States or Jamaica. Teachers working in collaboration with a larger body of interested stakeholders increases the likelihood that their work will be successful by placing teachers in roles where they are key actors in the critical process of analysis and transformation, not merely recipients of decrees handed down to them by others. Hyacinth Evans (2001) cited Paulo Freire (1973, 1985) with regard to power, agency, and criticality in action,

> Education should be for critical consciousness, serving to transform attitudes and beliefs internalized under a colonial or postcolonial system. The transformation serves to "emancipate" and empower the learners. In this context, the educator has a significant role to play, but that role requires a critical attitude on the part of the teacher. It also requires a critical pedagogy. (p. 148)

Evans (2001) went on to argue that "critical reflection and a critical pedagogy are essential in a post-colonial setting where there has been a denigration of black intelligence, black character, and black cultural forms" (p. 149). Of course, the reality is that as a group, teachers are generally treated as semi-professionals who are somehow undeserving of the respect and autonomy that is granted most other professionals. In the previous chapter, reference was made to work by Etzioni (1969), Lortie (1969, 1975), and Ingersoll and Merrill (2011) regarding teachers as semi-professionals and the problems associated with the professionalism and professional status of teachers. Related issues associated with gender, social class, and education also contribute to beliefs about the social status of teachers and their competency to make education related decisions. Teaching is still seen as women's work and the lack of status and compensation mirrors the low status of women in general society. In this book, I argue that without fundamental changes in the roles, processes, and products of teachers' work, the progress of school reform in Jamaican schools will be stymied; a system that is financially strapped and academically broken will continue to fail families and communities. Issues related to equity, advocacy, and social justice are irrelevant as long as schools are failing to successfully achieve minimal social, economic, and/or academic goals. Increased professional status is necessary for changes in teachers' work and the success of teacher leadership among Jamaican teachers. An understanding of four basic concepts is prerequisite to this discussion:

- the meaning of teacher leadership,
- the role of teacher advocacy and transformative leadership in school improvement,
- professional learning communities (PLCs) as a foundation for teacher professionalism, and
- leadership capacity building that involves all major stakeholders.

In this chapter, we will examine each of these concepts and apply them to teachers' work in Jamaica.

Teacher Leadership in Jamaica

Teacher leadership has been addressed in the research literature for many decades. The definitions may vary but the common elements are the same;

teacher leadership includes expanded notions about teaching, learning, and leading in schools, classrooms, and communities with teachers acting as learners, leaders, advocates and mentors in collaboration with major stakeholders. These roles can be both formal and informal. Silva et al. (2000) discussed the evolution of teacher leadership in terms of three waves: first, teachers as managers committed to increasing the efficacy of educational organizations; second, teachers were viewed as instructional specialists; and third, teachers as the primary directors of school culture. In earlier work, I proposed that the time is ripe for a fourth wave of teacher leadership where teachers assume roles (and work) as transformative leaders who are ideologically committed to creating educational spaces where the principles of social justice, equity, and equal access to the resources needed to address learning differences and difficulties are paramount (Blair, 2018b, p. 423). This fourth wave reflects a re-imagined view of both the nature of teachers' work and the role of teacher leadership in guiding school reform efforts that reflect the values and beliefs of diverse communities and honors the complexities of pedagogical decision-making. It is unfathomable to consider doctors and lawyers not having this kind of power in their professional work, and as such, teachers, who are equally important should be able to step into these roles in 21st century schools.

Katzenmeyer and Moller (2009) in their seminal work, *Awakening the Sleeping Giant: Helping Teachers Develop as Teacher Leaders,* suggest that teacher leaders are needed to "lead within and beyond the classroom; identify with and contribute to a community of teacher leaders and learners; influence others toward improved educational practices; and accept responsibility for achieving the outcomes of their leadership" (p. 6). The Center for Strengthening the Teaching Profession ([CSTP], 2009) defines teacher leadership as the "knowledge, skills and dispositions demonstrated by teachers who positively influence student learning by influencing adults, formally and informally, beyond individual classrooms" (p. 2). Both definitions emphasize that teacher leadership is about dispositions and influencing school improvement efforts not solving problems. CSTP goes even further by highlighting that effective teacher leadership is the intersection of knowledge and skills, positive dispositions, and the presence of roles and opportunities that give teacher leaders the chance to not only teach, but learn and lead (p. 1). These conditions for teacher leadership are important because teachers must make honest appraisals of their own strengths and weaknesses and evaluate what skills and knowledge are necessary to be good leaders. Having a willingness to use critical reflection to make personal evaluations as well as critique the larger context for one's work is essential. The dispositions of teacher leaders are equally important; teacher leaders must have integrity, efficacy, and content knowledge to be credible leaders among their peers and others (CSTP,

2009, p. 1). And finally, there must be roles and opportunities for teacher leaders. Administrators and Ministry officials must be proactive in working with teachers to identify the kinds of roles and opportunities that give teachers meaningful ways to impact all aspects of the pedagogical process as well as serve as advocates and mentors to novice teachers and less advantaged students. CSTP breaks down teacher leadership into specific skills: communication, collaboration, knowledge of content and pedagogy, working with adult learners, systems thinking and highlights a context for this work that is informed by an equity lens. A focus on the kinds of skills needed and areas of professional development that are prerequisite for effective leadership are essential. This is important because for many teachers, the prospect of being a teacher leader seems daunting at best, and at worst, a time-consuming and thankless job. In order to be successful, teacher leadership has to be integrated into the very fabric of teachers' work with time allocated for teacher leadership and professional development as well as an appropriate system of rewards that recognizes the work of teacher leaders.

Lambert (2003a) expands the work of teacher leadership to be inclusive of the kinds of tasks embodied by the expanded roles and responsibilities of teachers working to influence school improvement:

> Teacher leaders are those whose dreams of making a difference have either been kept alive or have been reawakened by engaging with colleagues and working within a professional culture.... Those for whom the dream has been kept alive are reflective, inquisitive, focused on improving their craft and action oriented; they accept responsibility for student learning and have a strong sense of self. They know their intentions well enough not to be intimidated into silence by others, are open to learning, and understand the three dimensions of learning in schools: student learning, the learning of colleagues, and learning of their own. (p. 33)

More important, and certainly applicable to Jamaica, is the suggestion:

> Within every school there is a "sleeping giant" of teacher leadership that can be a strong catalyst for making changes to improve student learning. By using the energy of teacher leaders as agents of school change, public education will stand a better chance of ensuring that "every child has a high quality of teacher." (Wehling, 2007, p. 14, as cited in Katzenmeyer & Moller, 2009, p. 2)

Teacher leadership becomes more important when you consider how it has the potential to not only impact school improvement but also strengthen the teaching profession. In schools with high levels of teacher leadership, multiple researchers have documented the presence of shared leadership, values and vision, collective and applied learning, supportive school culture and a deprivatization of teaching through shared practice, knowledge, and expertise (Danielson, 2006; Katzenmeyer & Moller, 2009; Lambert, 2003a). More importantly, teacher leadership leads to benefits that increase teacher retention and overall job satisfaction; for example, greater teacher efficacy, less resistance to change, expanded career opportunities, greater accountability, and increased influence, advocacy, and mentorship among teachers (Danielson, 2006; Katzenmeyer & Moller, 2009; Lambert, 1998, 2003a). Teacher leaders working as action researchers and constructivist learners should be on the "front line" in addressing the most tenacious educational problems; problem definition, data collection, and research used to construct new knowledge and apply it in novel ways to teaching and learning dilemmas. Berry (2019) provides evidence to support teacher development as constructivist learning:

> To develop teacher leaders, then, it's not enough just to appoint a few teachers to be instructional coaches, who provide others with one-to-one support. Rather, this kind of learning is more of a "socially distributed phenomena" that develops over time, among members of a group. As teachers gain efficacy, they must have opportunities to reflect on what they master in the context of structured collaboration. (Szczesiul & Huizenga, 2015, as cited in Berry, 2019, para. 21)

As constructivist learners, Lambert proposed a "reciprocal process of constructivist learning" wherein teachers engage in the following kinds of activities:

- *Surfacing:* What do we currently believe and do? Strengths and weaknesses. Mission, purpose, and vision statements.
- *Inquiry:* Conducting action research, observation, reading, discussion, research on best practices, data collection.
- *Dialogue and Reflection:* How do we make sense of prior assumptions and practices? What are we doing right? wrong? What are the obstacles to change?
- *Reframing:* How do we plan for action based on what we now know and understand? How will reshape, revision, and plan for transformation? (Lambert, 2003a, p. 22)

There are no problems in Jamaican schools that could not be positively impacted by teacher leaders and one of the best arguments for teacher leadership is that it does not require additional resources. The schools are already populated by teachers and administrators; harnessing this power on behalf of school improvements seems a win for everyone involved. Hence,

Katzenmeyer and Moller's (2009) references to this process as *Awakening a Sleeping Giant*. However, researchers are quick to acknowledge that despite the strengths of encouraging teacher leadership, there will be resistance:

> Why is engendering teacher leadership considered difficult by many principals and superintendents? Several reasons come to mind: a philosophy of leadership that situates leadership work within formal authority roles, a hierarchical view of authority and power, and an insistence that if we just find the right "carrot," the right incentive package, we can coax teachers to take on leadership roles. Such attitudes produce short term, shallow and unsustainable results. Old assumptions bind and confine. (Lambert, 2003b, p. 421)

In most schools, the role of the principal is important to overcoming resistance to teacher leadership and ensuring the success of teacher leaders. Just as teachers have to be forthright about their own beliefs about the roles of teachers, principals must acknowledge preconceived biases about successful schools. Roofe (2020) noted the following:

> The principal's stance, philosophy, leadership style, decision-making approaches, and relationship with staff will influence the culture created. Principals help to shape teachers' learning, motivation and working conditions. But school culture is not only influenced by the principal, though he or she is the main custodian. The culture of a school is also influenced by the relationships between principal and staff, teachers and teachers, teachers and students, students and students, with parents and with the community. (p. 80)

According to Roofe, complaints about a school ethos that doesn't support teacher leadership fall into three areas: first, hypocrisy in decision-making by the leaders; second, gender positioning by males for leadership positions; and third, the formation of teacher cliques in schools (p. 82). Lambert (2003a) proposes that a larger view of participation patterns and a focus on building a community of learners and leaders is a fundamental part of creating a school culture that nurtures leadership. She describes successful contexts for teacher leadership as having high leadership capacity: "broad-based, skillful participation in the work or leadership" (p. 4). Schools operating with high leadership capacity have the following characteristics:

- principal, teachers, parents, and students as skillful leaders;
- shared vision resulting in program coherence;
- inquiry-based use of data to inform decisions and practice;
- broad involvement, collaboration, and collective responsibility reflected in roles and actions;

- reflective practice that leads consistently to innovation; and
- high or steadily improving student achievement. (Lambert, 2003a, p. 5)

Schools with high leadership capacity reinforce a constructivist approach to learning and leading that is defined by attention to not only student learning but also to teacher learning and seeking to "achieving collective responsibility for the school and becoming a community of learners" (Lambert, 2003a, p. 3). Lambert (2003a) and Katzenmeyer and Moller (2009) suggest that professional learning communities (PLCs) are fundamental to efforts to build leadership capacity. Katzenmeyer and Moller define these as, "healthy contexts for teacher leadership" (pp. 8–9). The establishment of PLCs as a mechanism for promoting broad-based participation is an essential part of the community of learners and leaders model that Lambert proposes:

> A high leadership capacity school, therefore, involves broad-based, skillful participation in the work of leadership on the part of teachers as well as other school community members. Since leadership is defined as reciprocal, purposeful learning in community, such "work" embraces a shared vision, inquiry, dialogue, reflection and a focus on learning. Skillful participation in this work of leadership is more likely to result in a learning community, for educators who learn from each are more likely to lead. Hence a learning community is at the heart of a high leadership capacity school—they are parallel constructs. (Lambert, 2003b, p. 426)

Within these settings, teachers are learning in social contexts where teachers learn, share, and address problems as a group rather than individually. In this way, it is possible for teachers to move beyond the 2×4 model of teaching; for example, the two covers of a textbook, the four walls of the classroom; and embark on a journey to deprivatize teaching, and encourage teachers to open their classrooms for scrutiny, critique, and learning opportunities among other teachers.

Katzenmeyer and Moller (2009) describe schools that are professional learning communities possess the following dimensions:

1. Supportive and shared leadership,
2. Shared values and vision,
3. Collective learning and application of learning,
4. Supportive conditions,
5. Shared personal practice. (p. 8)

In this way, the process and product of teacher leadership is shaped by the continuous input of all stakeholders and there is regular negotiation of both teachers' work and the pedagogical approaches to school improvement.

Sustainability is a critical dimension of teacher leadership and school improvement. Lambert (2003a) advised that there are four conditions necessary for maintaining a school's capacity for leadership: "1. a sustained sense of purpose, 2. succession planning and selection, 3. enculturation, 4. a rhythm of development, and finally, 5. conversion of practice into policy" (p. 94). Lambert et al. (2016) note, "Sustainability is the crucial outcome of high leadership capacity" (p. 102). The importance of sustainability is also acknowledged by Katzenmeyer and Moller (2009) in their consideration of the importance of both growing and nurturing a body of teacher leaders within a school community in order to keep progress continuous and not chaotic and episodic:

> To rely on one leader in the school to maintain the momentum for innovation is risky because school systems transfer principals, key teachers retire or leave the system, and those remaining at the school are left to keep change moving forward.... A critical mass of teacher leaders can make a difference by taking responsibility for moving forward while the new leadership is established in the school. (p. 34)

It is important not to underestimate the power of building a school culture that facilitates the growth and development of teacher leadership as the norm and not the exception. A focus on the rewards of teacher leadership, both collective and individual, can become a tool for attracting teachers who might be reluctant to engage in teacher leadership as an important dimension of their work as teachers.

As another dimension of teachers' work, a reimagining of teachers as leaders requires that we acknowledge that teachers are able to articulate what "pulled" them to teaching; however, a frustration encountered by many teachers is the knowledge that their desires to change the world are not supported or appreciated in school communities where they have little power beyond their classrooms (Weiler, 1988). The importance of an ideological commitment to transformative teacher leadership cannot be underestimated. Teachers may not have the language to describe how teacher leadership infused with fundamental values can transform the parameters of teachers' work, but it is critical that a discussion of this facet of teaching not be ignored in efforts to improve schools by simply focusing on training and accountability. Noted author and researcher, Bettina Love (2019) gave birth to the idea of "abolitionist teaching" as a model for teachers' work that is infused with an ethical and moral dimension. She poignantly describes this ideological orientation in the following:

> Abolitionist teaching is choosing to engage in the struggle for educational justice knowing that you have the ability and human right to refuse oppres-

sion and refuse to oppress others, mainly your students. What does this approach look like in the classroom and beyond? Teachers working with community groups in solidarity to address issues impacting their students and their students' communities. Reimagining and rewriting curriculums with local and national activities to provide students with not only examples of resistance but also strategies of resistance. (p. 11)

Abolitionist teaching reimagines the roles of teachers and acknowledges a moral component of teachers' work that is often ignored and not subjected to critical inquiry. The work of teachers who are intellectuals and action researchers is, by necessity, informed by thinking about the intersection of pedagogical practices and the sources of oppression. Questions about who benefits and who loses when groups are denied access to knowledge, decision-making, and full professional status is an important part of the conversation. Teaching is a political act that recognizes the agency and power that resides in the work of individual teachers. Gary Anderson (2009) complements these ideas by expanding the notion of teacher leadership and teachers' work to include the idea of *advocacy leadership*; he discusses the relational possibilities of roles that work collaboratively and honor authenticity and mutual commitment to shared goals and purposes. He describes advocacy leadership in the following way:

> An advocacy leader believes in the basic principles of a high quality and equitable public education for all children and is willing to take risks to make it happen. Advocacy leaders tend to be skilled at getting beneath high-sounding rhetoric to the devil in the details. They are skeptical by nature. They know the difference between the trappings of democracy and the real thing. They refuse to collude in so-called collaborative teams or distributed leadership endeavors that are inauthentic...and yet, they draw an ethical line that cannot be crossed—not to be authoritarian, but to defend against the powerful using their power against the powerless. (pp. 14–15)

Katzenmeyer and Moller's (2009) ideas about teacher leadership taken in combination with Anderson's advocacy leadership provides a blueprint for teacher leadership that has the potential to lead to long-term meaningful school reform that is simultaneously grounded in the needs of both teachers and students and potentially, transformative. One could say that "teacher leaders acting as intellectual and moral provocateurs in the educational landscape" could transcend 21st century chaos and uncertainty (Blair, 2018b, p. 424).

Katzenmeyer and Moller (2009) provide a developmental model for teachers trying to understand how they can become teacher leaders. The model acknowledges developmental differences among teachers depending upon years of experience and personal responsibilities. It asks teachers to answer the following questions:

- Personal Assessment: "Who Am I?"
  - What are my strengths and developmental needs?
  - What are the behaviors, values, and philosophy that I value?
  - Do I self-monitor my own behavior for congruence between values and philosophy?
  - Do I regularly reflect on my practice and identify areas for improvement?
- Changing Schools: "Where Am I?"
  - dimensions of school culture
  - professional development and learning
  - environment
  - innovation and improvement
  - communication across multiple levels
  - decision-making
  - collaboration
- Influencing Strategies: "How Do I Lead?"
  - influencing strategies
    - listening skills
    - group skills
    - negotiating skills
    - how to prepare to influence others
      - your position
      - data
      - perspectives
      - options
      - agreement
- Planning for Action: "What Can I Do?"
  - current information
  - likelihood of achieving desired outcome
  - ideal situation
  - existing strategies
  - research and best practices
  - selected strategies and actions steps (pp. 101–117)

Using this model helps teachers working in collaboration with others to identify the issues and problems that impede school improvement and then make a plan for influencing and advocating for changes. These are not small things to consider. There are no easy answers to complicated problems, but never estimate the power of small groups of people collaborating and advocating for school success.

The Voices of Jamaican Teacher Leaders

I have worked with Jamaican teachers for almost 30 years. Much of the data that informs this book was gathered from surveys and interviews with Jamaican teachers who were participating in the Western Carolina University-Jamaica Program. Over a period of 3 years, at least 35 teachers from across the island (Kingston, Mandeville, Montego Bay, and Discovery Bay) completed the interviews for this study. Using qualitative tools of analysis, the responses were coded and organized by themes. These teachers, as a group, may be somewhat different in that they were already demonstrating a high level of commitment to the profession by being engaged in graduate studies; however, most were experienced practitioners with many years of "front line" experience in the classroom. As a group, these teachers have made incredible sacrifices to attend classes and complete a graduate degree with many of them overcoming tremendous obstacles that are both economic, personal, and professional. Most of the teachers who participated in my research consider themselves teacher leaders; however, few believe that they have any formal power or authority in decision-making. They note that while many things have changed through the years, others have not. Many roads are difficult to traverse and travel to school and to night classes is treacherous. Technology has transformed the island and classrooms; teachers (and students) have access to information that was previously difficult to locate, but Internet access is expensive and unreliable. Books and printed materials are more accessible but more expensive to acquire, but nevertheless, many of my students' access information through their mobile phones. As such, these students paint a picture of schools and classrooms where the work is hard, but their commitment to its importance is unwavering. Teachers responded to a short interview protocol that included the following questions:

1. Describe yourself as a teacher. How did you get here? Background? Education? Job Experiences?
2. Describe the school culture where you work. Identify those people and things that support your work. Identify those people and things that make your job more difficult.
3. Do you consider yourself a Teacher Leader? Why or Why not?
4. Describe the formal and informal processes that lead to decision-making in your school. What roles do teachers play? Administrators? How are people held responsible/accountable for implement-

ing decisions? What role do you play in decision-making? How is this similar or different from other teachers?
5. How do you define teacher expertise? What is the teacher culture at your school for teachers to use their knowledge and expertise? How are various levels of expertise utilized? How does expertise afford your involvement in decision making? (Adapted from Acker-Hocevar et al., 2012).

Teacher responses support Roofe's (2020) ZRESS model of the character traits of teacher leaders; they were overwhelmingly zealous, resilient, eager, self-evaluative and solutions oriented. An analysis of major themes and concerns produced four categories of information, school culture, decision-making, teachers' work and expertise and personal power, and advocacy and social justice.

Teachers value their relationships with students and the pursuit of academic excellence is important; however, teachers regularly express concern regarding the social and emotional development of their students who come from challenging economic environments. While a majority of Jamaican teachers are female, most schools and officials with the ministry are male. Power relationships are interesting in that they reflect a level of gender bias towards women despite the fact that Jamaican women are generally much more accomplished academically than men; statistics regularly show large achievement gaps between boys and girls that extend into higher education. Again, despite the problems that come with a teaching career, most teachers enthusiastically declare their allegiance to the students and the communities where they work.

School Culture

School culture is regularly discussed by Jamaican teacher leaders. Their issues and concerns varied, but school climate and school culture have a big impact on overall satisfaction and motivation in teachers' work. The following excerpt from one participant is long, but offers a powerful view into the daily struggles of an experienced teacher:

> The culture at the school that I worked at for 7 years was often rooted in struggle and defeat. I worked at a "mission possible," Title I, and underperforming (failing—when grades were given to schools) school. We had many students coming to us in 6th grade or transferring in that were many years behind in reading and math skills and lacking key social and emotional skills. Many teachers were overly negative, had low expectations of students, poor opinions of leadership and little hope for improvement. There were however

a few leaders within each content area and grade level that had proven themselves through hard work, high quality instruction, high value-added data, and dedication to improving the school. Unfortunately, 5 teachers that I can think of now that made the largest impacts on me and our school when I first started teaching have now become administrators, or transferred to higher performing schools. When these teachers worked at my school, they led initiatives, shared ideas and resources, had professional and positive attitudes and behaviors and were well respected amongst others.

For those individuals that made my job more difficult, they were very unreliable, would come to PLCs unprepared, unwilling to work together, had negative attitudes, and were easily agitated and confrontational. Teacher absences was a major issue at our school as teachers often handled absences unprofessionally by not notifying others when they would be out, not providing lesson plans for substitutes, not trying to locate a substitute and not communicating when they thought they would be returning. The burden often fell on other teachers, or those teachers with more flexible schedules such as instructional coaches and/or special education teachers.

As administration changed, the culture would slowly shift to include more solidarity, positive attitudes, and determination, which would only last a short while. On average, we lost about 5–7 teachers during a school year as they quit teaching, transferred to other schools, or changed careers. We often had another 3–5 teachers that regularly (i.e., weekly) called out sick from work. Hard working teachers began to feel overworked, as they were called on to help out and fill in these gaps as needed. We had about 30% teacher turnover each year. (JM50-22)

Other teachers describe similar struggles in their work as teacher leaders.

We have recently changed principals at my school therefore the school climate and culture shifted a little. This new principal brought his own style of leadership and there is a power struggle now. Both administrators and academic staff are trying their best to be out of each other space. Teachers teaching while principal is trying to figure his way out in his new community. (JM2-22)

There are a lot of great teachers at the institution where I work but I have realized that persons just do the minimum. Only one set of teachers are constantly asked to do certain things, serve on committees etc. (JM5-22)

I am presently employed at a co-ed school, with a population of 1,200 students. The teachers are a mixture of personality and different working attitudes. At present we have trailblazers, pioneers, setters, stay at home and the saboteurs. Sometimes the saboteurs are the loudest because they tend to want to discourage the trailblazers and the pioneer. Saboteurs are always finding faults in what we do and they are never ready to help yet they have all the opinions. (JM16-19)

62 ▪ *Jamaican Teachers, Jamaican Schools*

> The school where I work; the culture is a developing one and depending on who you asked they may give you various opinions of what the culture is however, for me it is a culture of policy pusher that often doesn't reach to the intended target; the students on a consistent basis, and as a result there is a disconnect between administration to teachers and teachers to students so the school will be running well then another time not so well politely putting it. Because the school is transitioning from one principal to another there are a few teachers that are resisting change and acting as saboteur to the school operations, the school perimeter fencing is a safety threat and there are many open areas that persons can enter school to carry out vandalism, attacks and rubbery and easily escape in the bushes and there a few students who really do not want to conform to school rules and regulations and they also make teaching and learning very challenging for teachers and other students. (JM14-21)

> The school culture at the institution where I work seems to be very competitive. However I believe that most of the teachers are focused and believe in the students hence they try and find creative means of ensuring that the students learn. I believe however that you have to know who you are as an individual because if you lose sight of that then you won't survive at this institution. I am not the most talkative person but I am a hard worker. There are very few persons such as my grade supervisor, one of the vice principals and some of my colleagues who have congratulated me on my work ethics and have asked me to host professional development sessions and so on. However, I don't really get that same reception from the principal. She operates on the basis where you are volunteered into certain positions or told that you will start serving in a new position. I don't particularly like this form of leadership. I prefer a school culture where each person is respected and their skills valued. (JM5-22)

> The culture of the school I currently work, can be described as different as the educators are of a competitive and dedicated nature. It's a very big school, having over one thousand four hundred (1,400) students enrolled, envied and lauded for its maintained high level of academic achievements. Often described as a school family is the knitting of both academic and ancillary staff, who not only seek to do their jobs but does it with the same goal of ensuring that our students and their needs are always priority. (JM1-22)

School culture is regularly described as one of the most important aspects of teachers' work and central to school improvement. Katzenmeyer and Moller (2009) identify school culture as a key feature in the work of teacher leaders. Without a positive school culture and a supportive administrator, it is unlikely that teacher leadership or PLCs will thrive. Levin and Schrum (2017) note that while school culture and school climate are often used interchangeably, school climate is subsumed under the culture of the work environment (p. 77). Brown (2004) identifies many important dimensions of school culture, but some of those characteristics that reflect the concerns expressed by Jamaican teachers are the following:

Jamaican Teachers and Schools ▪ 63

- sufficient time for teachers and students to do their work well;
- leadership that encourages and protects trust, on-the-job learning, flexibility, risk-taking, innovation, and adaptation to change;
- data-driven decision-making systems that draw on timely, accurate, qualitative and quantitative information about progress toward the vision and sophisticated knowledge about organizational change;
- unwavering support from parents; and
- district flexibility and support for multiple school designs, visions, missions and innovations (p. 4).

Clearly, a focus on time, leadership, risk-taking, flexibility, and support should be a part of any major consideration of school culture and school change. In this way, understanding and critiquing school culture provides a context for answering Katzenmeyer and Moller's questions about changing schools and discussing, "Where Am I?"

Decision-Making

As previously discussed, Jamaican teachers are better educated than ever before in their history; a bachelor's degree is the expectation for most teachers and a master's degree is encouraged. However, despite these changes, the power structure in most schools is hierarchical with most teachers falling near the bottom. For example, the following chart was drawn by one of the teachers I interviewed describing the "chain of command" at her school:

Principal and Vice Principals
⬇
Vice Principals
⬇
Senior Management Team
⬇
Teachers
⬇
Assistants Teachers
⬇
Ancillary Workers (JM5-22)

Based on what I see, decision making is really done by the principal. The vice principals may have a say to some extent. The senior management team can make decisions relating to their cluster but in some event based on the severity of the issue they have to report it to the vice principal. (JM5-22)

There is however room for improvement as some teachers do not completely trust administrators and do not always feel like they have their best interest at heart. Due to the school being private and the parents being quite influential, some teachers feel like administrators side with the parents instead of advocating for their teachers. This may be the case in some scenarios but they also do advocate for teachers too. The level of trust between this group and the need for an HR department to help manage these situations is definitely an area of improvement. (JM6-22)

The administrators at the school had an open-door policy with its teachers. However, in the last year the school has a new principal. Even though he adopted this open-door policy; only selected teachers use this approach as the new principal isn't as laid back as the previous where teachers could regularly convey their concerns. With this new principal, all decisions stop with him. Whenever teachers have any concern they liaison their concerns to their grade supervisors or their coordinators; who then takes feedback to the teachers. A few of the supervisors are vocal when it comes on to issues that affects them, however a majority of them complies because they don't want to be labelled as being difficult. (JM7-22)

The principal along with the chairman makes most decisions at my place of work especially where policies are concerned. Senior teachers and grade coordinators are placed on several committees which includes: sports, events, fundraising etc to discuss activities throughout the school year. The senior teachers then gives the principal an update; decisions are usually made here too, then the senior teacher takes feedback to the junior teachers. (JM7-22)

Most decisions are made by the administrators however, teachers are given an opportunity to share their ideas then seek approval from the administrators to implement any proposed changes. (JM6-22)

Most major decisions regarding curriculum, scheduling, and instruction is decided by the head principal with some contributing feedback from assistant principals and some teacher leaders. Teachers have the opportunities to contribute ideas and concerns for decisions making in school improvement team meetings, where mostly teacher leaders at grade level and subject areas participate. For grade level concerns, lead teachers for each subject area have some influence on decisions that are made, however the grade level designated assistant principal makes the majority of the decisions. Grade level assistant principals often listen to lead teachers on the grade level as they often have more experience with certain situations (e.g., scheduling, grouping students). (JM50-22)

As a professional, authority and autonomy in decisions regarding the what, how, and why of one's work are part of the defining features of one's identity. Not only do Jamaican teachers have little voice in broader discussions and decision-making regarding the schools, teachers also have limited input in policies established for curriculum, behavior, and even teaching philosophy and style. The semi-professional status of teachers is regularly reinforced when major decisions are handled by administrators who have little firsthand knowledge of the content and circumstances of teachers' work in the various parishes. Lambert's (2003a) emphasis on building leadership capacity in schools focuses on "broad-based, skillful participation in the work of leadership" (p. 4). Again, high performing schools are characterized by high levels of skillful participation in decision-making; the involvement of *all* major stakeholders is an important prerequisite for healthy contexts for the work of school leaders. However, low performing schools reflect a lack of skillful participation by major stakeholders and decision-making is inevitably top-down and authoritarian. The school culture in these schools is neither healthy nor satisfying for those who work in these settings.

Teachers' Work and Expertise

The professional status of teachers is closely linked to views about their work and expertise. The teachers in this study overwhelmingly described themselves as leaders and their knowledge of content and pedagogy was demonstrated in their educational accomplishments and work experience. Many of these teachers believe that their expertise is recognized and utilized; however, many others believe that it is not.

> Teacher expertise comes from an exceptional understanding of content, how students acquire this knowledge, and ways to effectively engage students in the curriculum. Expert teachers know multiple ways to deliver content and find ways to address the needs and varying levels of abilities of all students. Within the school that I worked at, teachers' expertise was valued and supported by administration and other teachers. Teachers that displayed expertise were used as models for others, and often utilized to support other teachers in the building with less experience. Teachers with greater expertise were given varying leadership opportunities, and professional development opportunities. Teachers with higher levels of expertise were often given more influence in decision making and asked to participate in committees that often made decisions or planned initiatives or programs for improvement. Teachers with more expertise were often asked to officially "mentor" beginning teacher level staff. Additionally, teachers were often strategically placed on grade levels or teams to provide a balance in experience, skills, and expertise. Less experienced teachers were encour-

aged to participate in at least 1 major school committee, as this provided opportunities for input and growth. (JM50-22)

Teachers are sometimes frustrated as they feel their opinion doesn't matter. They believe that teachers with personal relationships with administration get approval over them. Teachers whose ideas are not supported tend to be less likely to participate in school events. The same set of teachers tend to participate in all events planned or held at the school. (JM15-22)

Due to a lack of resources at my school the teachers who are experts in their fields are not utilized as they should within my school community. These teachers are placed into the general classroom and are only utilized if need be. Whenever given the chance to display their expertise on selected topics, they do not get the support that is expected from their colleagues as oftentimes it comes off as bragging. (JM7-22)

Based on what I see, decision making is really done by the principal. The vice principals may have a say to some extent. The senior management team can make decisions relating to their cluster but in some event based on the severity of the issue they have to report it to the vice principal. Teachers may make decisions in their class but honestly speaking I get the advice from my supervisor on most matters. What I have come to notice at this institution is that teachers have no serious allies. (JM5-22)

As previously discussed, Jamaican teachers are passionate and committed. All of the teachers who participated in this study are graduate students pursuing advanced degrees in education; many have expressed a desire to do doctoral level work. Many of the recent recommendations of task forces on education reference a need for professional development, but absent from these mandates is any discussion of utilizing highly skilled and accomplished teachers in this planning or implementation (Jamaican Education Transformation Commission, 2022). At a minimum, any discussion of promoting teacher leadership in Jamaica must include a plan for acknowledging and elevating the knowledge and expertise of teachers.

Personal Power, Advocacy, and Social Justice

Finally, an important component of teacher leadership is personal power and agency. While personal power or the lack thereof is often demonstrated in decision-making, it is more complicated. Personal power extends to a sense of control in one's relationships and work in both the classroom and the workings of various departments and programs. Decisions about advocacy and social justice are a source of power in these relationships. Acker-Hocevar and Touchton (1999) discussed agency and power within the context of the social relationships within a school. They suggested that "responsibility and accountability may rest on the internal processes in the school to enable or 'empower' teachers to take a legitimate role in their school's development" (p. 3). Teachers are critical to the promotion of values and beliefs aligned with advocacy and social justice for children. Power and agency in personal practice is an important dimension of professional status, and as such, a part of teachers' work that is critical but seldom discussed in relationship to teachers' work in Jamaica.

> Because the school is small, requests and suggestions regarding teaching and learning are made directly to the principal for considerations. Other matters are directed to the senior teacher who consults with the principal for a decision. However, teachers are allowed to make decisions that affect their individual classes. (JM19-19)

> Administrators hold the power. Teachers are free to voice their opinion however no action may be taken based on teachers' opinion. (JM15-22)

> This job however, can be demanding, requiring some teachers to carry out numerous responsibilities that can result in teachers feeling burnout and a sense that no one cares. (JM4-22)

> The power relationships within your school between different groups such as teachers and administrators are very lineal. Teachers think these relationships do not encourage them and so most teachers leave at the first opportunity. (JM8-22)

> Many teachers, however, feel like their opinions are heard but not necessarily accepted and used. (JM4-22)

> As was stated above, the most power within the institution lies with the administration. However, based on observation and discussions with other colleagues some persons are willing to work with the administration but there are other teachers who are set in their ways and it doesn't matter what is said to them or who speaks to them they will not conform. I have split views on this as I believe that it stems from 2 areas: (a) how the administration deals with teachers has a lot to do with how some of these teachers behave; (b) some teachers don't care for your position or title, they will do what they want to do. (JM5-22)

> Most of the teachers at my school display a sense of motherhood or protection for the students beyond the formal setting. (JM2-22)

> Administration was clearly the head of power within our school. In my last year, there was a slight shift with teachers taking more control of important issues, decision making and implementing programs, however most teachers at our school knew that the power resided with administration. This was often displayed with student discipline, as when students were referred to administration for major issues, teachers had little input on solutions, or ideas. Teachers needed to combat this by taking matters into their own

hands, as often students removed from class were returned right back within the period or the next and the student continued to display similar behaviors. Additionally, decisions regarding coverage for absent teachers, scheduled changes (due to testing, etc.), and meetings, were often determined by administrators. Teachers had little power or influence over these decisions. It is important to note that certain teachers did appear to have more power (and support) than others. (JM-22)

My opportunities to use power helped to advocate for social justice for students with disabilities and often towards students with limited English proficiency who were often placed in "inclusion" classes with students with and without disabilities for additional supports. When possible, I would use my influence and position to ensure that these students were appropriately placed and given proper and timely modifications and/or accommodations.

Additional I would like to share that the profession is currently in a state of transition, which I would deem as from traditional methods of teaching to modernized 21st century. With this said, as educators we have to be abreast with technological methodologies to cater to the needs of the varied types of learners as well as adapt to the modes that will promote and achieve academic success. (JM1-22)

I have a high value and emphasis towards showing all students compassion and giving them adequate supports and opportunities to succeed. I believe that students with behavior and academic challenges need the highest levels of support and encouragement, and traditional measures will not work for some. It takes a collaborative team effort to support some of our students and going it alone can be ineffective and debilitating. I have found that some teachers agree with this and will try just about anything to support certain students while other teachers stick to strict and traditional approaches towards all students and assume that some can cut it, and some cannot. I believe that administrators at our school want to give each child a chance and genuinely want them to succeed, however they are not always sure how to do this. (JM50-22)

I am an advocate for the children I work with. I strongly believe that there is always a reason for a bad behaviour. I have built a relationship with students in and outside of my class; this allows students who want to talk to someone they trust to come to me. Here they are guided and it also creates a safe space for them to feel heard and appreciated. (JM7-22)

I believe that students need someone in their corner, at times they may be hard to deal with however there is good in everyone and everyone deserves second choices. I valued my personal time with the students, I enjoy the relationship that I share with them. I am grateful that I am there to provide help and a listening ear for them. I am there to encourage, enable students and to give them a voice where it's needed. (JM16-19)

I advocate and promote social justice for especially children who may be falling behind due to developmental challenges or economic situations. I work to prevent discrimination of children by ensuring that welfare support is handled discretely and to see to it that children are treated fairly. (JM19-19)

Teachers' voices demonstrate that power, advocacy, and social justice are important to their work; they advocate for their students' needs even when they personally have no one advocating for teachers' needs and concerns. Little (1988) proposed that the success of teacher leadership will depend on how schools address five related issues:

- understanding the work that teachers do
- the symbolic role that teacher leaders assume: helping and collaborating not fixing
- the agreements for getting started and working together as professionals
- incentives and rewards that favor collaboration
- the policies that connect the leadership work of teachers and administrators. (as cited in Berry, 2019)

Little gives us a point of departure for critiquing teachers' work and thinking about where it is and where it needs to be, but there has to be a general consensus among a majority of stakeholders that this process is important, needed, and necessary for overall school improvement. Berry (2019) suggested that "teacher leadership won't really take off until school leadership programs (in universities, districts, and nonprofits) begin to prepare teachers and principals *together*. Only by experiencing authentic collaboration with teachers can administrators become confident in teachers' capacity to lead and in their own ability to cultivate teachers' leadership skills" (para. 30). Teacher leaders working in collaboration with principals and Ministry officials represent a powerful influence in any plan for working with teachers to address the problems of Jamaican schools, but there has to be buy-in that teachers will be both the inspiration and motivation for initiating a collaborative process. Constituent groups are already working to address educational issues but the work is random and frequently uncoordinated. Working collaboratively is the only way to ensure that the best minds and talent will be working together in unison toward common goals and purposes. When thinking about this kind of collaboration, I consider the idea that "the whole is greater than the sum of the parts" (Aristotle). Teachers, administrators, Ministry officials, and other education leaders working in isolation to one another often generate random and unrelated solutions to problems, but working together they have major stakeholder involvement and broad-based investment in long-term, sustainable solutions.

70 ▪ Jamaican Teachers, Jamaican Schools

Berry believes that there are reasons to be optimistic about the progress of teacher leadership:

> Consider four developments that bode well for teacher leadership in the years ahead: (1) evidence on the positive effects of teacher leadership continues to mount, (2) increasingly, local and state policies are codifying and recognizing teacher leadership, (3) teacher leaders are becoming more proficient at using educational technology and sharing their expertise through digital media, and (4) researchers are deepening their knowledge about how teachers learn to lead effectively. (para. 5)

Teacher leadership does work; and as such, it is critical that the voices of Jamaican teachers be front and center of every reform report on education and schooling on the island. To do any less is an abhorrent relinquishing of responsibility for the well-being of Jamaica's schools and the future of education in the 21st century. Questions that might be considered for discussion are the following:

1. Are the voices of the teachers in this chapter reflective of the needs and concerns of all teachers across the island? How? What is missing?
2. Are Jamaican teachers ready and willing to be teacher leaders? What are the obstacles? What are the benefits?
3. Does abolitionist teaching, advocacy leadership, and transformative roles for teachers have a place in the work of educational leaders?
4. Is it possible for PLCs to serve as a foundation for teacher professionalism in Jamaican schools? What kind of support is needed to support these practices and avoid the establishment of cliques?
5. Who are the major stakeholders in any school community? Is there a general understanding and commitment to broad-based participation in the work of schools? Why or why not?

5

Jamaican Teachers, Jamaican Schools

Disrupting the Narrative

> *Do not get lost in a sea of despair. Be hopeful, be optimistic. Our struggle is not the struggle of a day, a week, a month, or a year, it is the struggle of a lifetime. Never, ever be afraid to make some noise and get in good trouble, necessary trouble.*
> —John Lewis (2018)

I think it is time for Jamaican teachers to make some noise and get in good trouble, necessary trouble. Christopher Emdin, *Teaching and Being Ratchetdemic* (YouTube video) talks about "rainbows over the 'hood'" (Emdin, 2018, 14:19). "Rainbows don't care where you are or where you come from.... rainbows just need the perfect conditions to allow its brilliance to be expressed; it cares not where it happens.... rainbows can hover over projects" (Emdin, 2018, 14:19). His belief that rainbows are not selective and that beauty can be found in any context is powerful. And that perspective can be compelling because our beliefs shape our view of the context and culture where we spend our days. Beliefs can empower and lead to positive action or they can demean, marginalize, and relegate one to a position of resignation and survival. Rainbows are beautiful and seldom do they not make us pause and take a second glance at what would otherwise be an ordinary view of the sky. I would suggest that Jamaican teachers need to take that second look and see that rainbow over their schools and seek practices and ways of being and doing teachers' work that makes their lives richer and their schools places of joy and success where magic can be created on a daily basis. Emdin introduces the notion of "ratchet," to discuss a "marriage of hip hop and academic behavior in academic settings" (Emdin, 2018, 9:25). Focusing on a "come as you are" thinking and an emphasis on authenticity and identity; credentials may be important, but passion and excitement are key to successful teachers *and* students. Emdin summarizes this in the following:

- I will not hide my ratchet self to make a broken system powerful.
- I will not be made to be less than because I choose to be myself.
- I will not judge brilliance by how I think it looks or sounds.
- I will be equally as ratchet as academic.
- Oreo no more. I will teach and be ratchetdemic. (Emdin, 2018, 13:35)

While Emdin's words may not resonate with teachers working in relatively conservative institutions. It is possible that these ideas can provide inspiration to new ways of thinking about the brilliance and talents of both teachers and students in Jamaica, and a consideration of the ways that Jamaican schools might change to accommodate their cultural diversity and create public educational spaces that support multiple images of the Jamaican identity and its cultural heritage.

Teacher Leadership as Teachers' Work

In many ways, teacher leadership is both a phenomenon and a mindset regarding the values, beliefs, and attitudes that guide teachers' work. As such, it has the potential to radically transform a beleaguered profession while also providing for the creation of educational spaces that allow for multiple ideologies to coexist and provide multifaceted definitions of efficacy in teaching and learning. Changing perceptions of teachers' work are paramount to efforts to move the teaching profession towards higher professional status and autonomy; a position that facilitates the emergence of teacher leadership. However, many of these changes must come from both within the profession and from shifting public perceptions that are reflected in the changing bureaucratic and political hierarchies that govern the organization and authority of teachers' work. Key to these efforts is an understanding on the part of all major stakeholders that the work of teachers is the bedrock of school reform; reform that begins with an acknowledgement that the unique knowledge, skills, and pedagogical understandings of teachers are essential to a transformation of schools and classrooms in the 21st century. In reality, teachers and teacher educators may be the only ones capable of articulating a vision for public education that has the potential for guiding our thinking about teachers' work in realistic, but important ways; a vision that by necessity must be informed both by ideology but also pragmatic concerns about unique student needs that are grounded in a commitment that is shaped by a moral and ethical dimension. Somewhere, however, that vision must intersect with institutions and hierarchies that facilitate broad-based and skillful support and provide opportunities for the translation of knowledge and beliefs into action. And somehow, this vision must recognize the life and energy can potentially be infused into schools today through an honoring of school reform demands that recognize and actively address the need to educate *all* children *all* of the time in *all* schools. When thinking about teachers and their relationships to reform efforts, a quote from the prologue of Tyack and Cuban (1995), *Tinkering Toward Utopia: A Century of Public School Reform*, sets the stage for a consideration of the tasks before us:

> Change where it counts the most—in the daily interactions of teachers and student—is the hardest to achieve and the most important, but we are not pessimistic about improving the public schools... To do this requires not only political will and commitment but also an accurate understanding of schools as institutions.... We favor attempts to bring about such improvements by working from the inside out, especially by enlisting the support and skills of teachers as key actors in reform.... Policy talk about educational reform has been replete with extravagant claims for innovations that flickered and faded. This is a pie-in-the sky brand of utopianism, and it has often led to disillusionment among teachers and to public cynicism. Exaggeration has pervaded these public rituals of dismay and promise. There is, however, a different kind of utopianism—a vision of a just democracy—that has marked the best discourse about educational purpose over the past century. We believe that debate over educational and social goals has become radically restricted in the past generation. An essential political task today is to renegotiate a pluralistic conception of the public good, a sense of trusteeship that preserves the best of the past while building generous conceptions of a common future. (p. 10)

All teachers must be stewards promoting the "public good," but they must also recognize the compelling reasons why they must be leaders promoting the idea that *how we define the problem determines the solution.* Low student achievement and low test scores are symptoms of the problems in public education. However, the "real" problems have much more to do with poverty and racism and the marginalization of families and children who are not representative of the White, Anglo-Saxon, protestant ideals. While Jamaica is not by any stretch of the imagination a White, Anglo-Saxon nation, the imposition of British values and beliefs through colonization is evident throughout the education system. Solving the "real" problems will not be simple; there are no "one size fits all" solutions for poverty and racism and marginalization, so policymakers, instead, have committed vast amounts of time, energy, and resources to a political solution for complex social problems: testing and accountability measures that focus on high stakes testing have dominated discussions of school reform. As long as teacher leadership is seen merely as a "tool" for fixing the unexamined problems associated with school improvement and accountability, the roles and responsibilities of teachers will be limited by governing bodies and groups with more power, but less knowledge about the problems in 21st century schools and classrooms.

I am confident that a serious reconsideration of teachers' work and the roles and functions of teacher leaders will produce mandates that teacher voices be central to all dialogue and discussion of school reform, and that simultaneously, teachers will have access to key positions responsible for defining the problems and determining the solutions in public education. Inevitably, these changes would result in meaningful, substantive changes; changes that would affect every facet of teachers' work, and most importantly, school improvement efforts.

Teachers as Transformative Intellectuals

Most educational scholars understand that the problems in public education are deeply ingrained in the debates about the form, process, and products of schooling that have dominated the public schools since independence; the problems are resilient and resistant to easy solutions. These problems will require smart teachers doing smart things. Giroux (1988) argues, "Teachers should become transformative intellectuals if they are to educate students to be active, critical citizens" (p. 127). And herein lies the most important issue, the "problems" that exist in schools today are not just teaching and learning issues that can be solved through task force reports and new policies and regulations. The "real problems" have a lot to do with teachers who are well-educated, but seldom given the authority to operate as intellectual decision-makers. As transformative intellectuals, teachers would be prepared at every level, both preservice and inservice, to assume roles as researchers and scholars as well as educational practitioners who have the tools needed to analyze and design classrooms and schools that facilitate critical thought and action while recognizing that teaching and learning are endeavors that require that these environments are structured in such a way that they are responsive to a constantly changing milieu. According to Giroux (1988), "Central to the category of transformative intellectual is the necessity of making the pedagogical more political and the political more pedagogical" (p. 127). His discussion concludes with the idea that "transformative intellectuals need to develop a discourse that unites the language of critique with the language of possibility, so that social educators recognize they can make changes. In doing so, they must speak out against economic, political, and social injustices both within and outside of schools" (p. 128). As a teacher educator, I daily confront the chasm between preparing graduate students to teach in traditional school environs or teaching teachers as intellectuals who will enter teaching with a well-defined vision for their roles as teachers, a vision infused with hope and possibilities that will guide the choices and decisions they make as educational leaders. In this way, teacher leadership is redefined and represents a radical repositioning of conversations about teachers' work and teacher leadership.

Even today, it is still important for us to reconsider questions regarding *how* and why teachers' work exists in its present form, but more importantly, we need to consider a different conceptual framework that has the potential to redirect *how* we think about teachers' work and *what* teachers' work might look like in 21st century schools and classrooms. Understanding teachers' work as being situated in political arenas where teachers are accountable for more than simply teaching and testing, but rather, where an important dimension of their work is advocacy leadership on behalf of both students and their parents must be a part of this critique. It is only in this manner that teaching will truly be responsive to the changing needs of a global society that will require schools to expand beyond the boundaries of individual classrooms, school buildings, and even local communities.

Teaching as a Profession

As previously noted, Jamaican teachers have more in common with semi-professionals than full-fledged professionals like nurses, doctors, or lawyers. Lortie (1969, 1975), Etzioni (1969), and Ingersoll and Merrill (2011) have discussed the problems with considering teaching a profession, and both have agreed that calling teaching a semi-profession is a more accurate designation based on the status of teachers; Jamaica's teachers, by virtue of their low status and lack of autonomy meet the criteria of semi-professionals. Jamaican teachers have a long history of limited educational credentials, low status, and even lower pay, but while there are increasing changes in the expectations for teacher preparation and practice, few school reforms recommend changes that would impact the professional status of teachers' work. Long considered a "women's profession," teachers have been subject to all of the inequities and biases associated with gender. Teachers are typically granted limited authority to make decisions beyond their classrooms and even in their classrooms they are expected to follow strict guidelines for the curriculum and student behavior. Opportunities to progress to leadership roles and responsibilities are closely guarded and often preference is granted to less experienced male colleagues. When one considers the characteristics that define a profession, it is clear that for most of recent history, teachers have fallen short. According to Ingersoll and Collins (2018), "These, of course, are not the only characteristics used to define professions, nor are they the only kinds of criteria used to distinguish or to classify work and occupations in general. But they are among the most widely used indicators of professions and professionals and are the subject of much discussion in reference to teachers and schools (p. 201). Central to this discussion is the fact that teachers today are better educated than at any other time in history; and yet, antiquated ideas about teachers' work have been slow to change. Despite changes in the educational credentials of teachers, teachers' work is still strictly defined within the narrow margins of traditional expectations regarding the role of teachers. Increased professional status is a necessary prerequisite to the promotion of teacher leadership as the norm in 21st century Jamaican schools. Table 5.1 compares typical definitions of a profession to those of present-day teacher leaders and proposes the kinds of reforms necessary for Jamaican teachers to assume their roles as full-fledged professionals.

The changes necessary for Jamaican teachers to begin to function as professionals are relatively small but significant. These changes focus on the roles, processes, and products of a reimagined profession. A familiarity by key Jamaican educational leaders with the ways in which teachers currently function and the kinds of issues that must be addressed in order to impact the roles, processes, and products of teachers' work is necessary if teacher leadership is to become the norm for Jamaican teachers.

Teacher Leadership and the Pandemic

The previous chapter highlighted conceptions of teachers' work and teacher leadership expressed by Jamaican teachers. The themes that emerged are consistent with the research completed by York-Barr and Duke (2004) summarizing common assertions related to key elements of teacher leadership. Relevant examples are the following:

Jamaican Teachers, Jamaican Schools ▪ 77

TABLE 5.1 Professional Characteristics: Jamaican Teachers and School Reform

Characteristics of a Profession (Ornstein, 1977, pp. 139–143)	Jamaican Teachers	Jamaican Teachers as Professionals
A defined body of knowledge learned in universities or professional schools.	Teaching requires at a minimum a 2-year diploma program with an internship.	Reforms requiring a bachelor's degree as a minimum qualification. Graduate degrees encouraged. Knowledge and expertise of teachers formally recognized.
Research and theory encouraged and combined with practice.	Research and theory limited. Curricular and pedagogical decisions made at higher levels.	Teacher training grounded in research and best practices. Teachers as action researchers who collect and apply data and research to effective educational practices. Personal accountability is an integral part of teachers' work. Teacher role includes defining of advocacy and social justice goals.
Control over licensing standards and entry requirements.	No control over licensing standards and entry requirements.	Establishment of professional boards that address credentialing and handle complaints. Teachers determine membership of board.
A code of ethics familiar to members so as to guide policy and behavior.	Code of ethics from Jamaican Teachers' Association (JTA)	Code of Ethics widely distributed and enforced. Teachers determine content of code of ethics and consequences for violations.
Professional reference groups providing standards of judgment and conduct.	Jamaican Teachers' Association (JTA)	JTA as a union with the power to represent teachers in negotiations with the Ministry of Education and Youth.
Administrators facilitating the work of professionals.	Administrators function in hierarchical roles. Top-down decision-making.	Administrators function as constructivist leaders in conjunction with teachers. Professional learning communities and practices associated with leadership capacity building are the norm. All major stakeholders involved in relevant decision-making.
Autonomy in determining one's own work.	Limited autonomy. Decision-making limited to classroom decisions.	Teachers responsible for all pedagogical decision-making. Formal structures established for policies, processes, and products of curriculum planning.
High commitment to work.	High levels of commitment.	High levels of commitment, enthusiasm, and motivation to teaching and school improvement.
Prestige associations and elite groups that carry weight.	Limited prestige and status.	Increased prestige and status. Recognition of teacher knowledge and expertise.
High status and economic standing.	Low status. Low levels of compensation.	Increased status, power, and recognition. Mediated entry into the profession that recognizes credentials and experience. Increased compensation.

- Teacher leadership is an umbrella term that includes a wide variety of work at multiple levels in education systems, including work with student, colleagues, and administrators and work that is focused on instruction, professional and organizational development.
- Teacher leaders have backgrounds as accomplished teachers, and they are respected by their colleagues. From the background, they extend their knowledge, skills, and influence to others in their school communities.
- Teacher leadership roles are often ambiguous. The likelihood of being successful as a teacher leader is increased if roles and expectations are mutually shaped and negotiated by teacher leaders, their colleagues, and principals on the basis of context-specific (and changing) instructional and improvement needs.
- Professional norms of isolation, individualism, and egalitarianism challenge the emergence of teacher leadership. Teachers who lead tend to feel conflict and isolation as the nature of their collegial relationships shift from primarily horizontal to somewhat hierarchical.
- Developing trusting and collaborative relationships is the primary means by which teacher leaders influence their colleagues.
- Principals play a pivotal role in the success of teacher leadership by actively supporting the development of teachers, by maintaining open channels of communication, and by aligning structures and resources to support the leadership work of teachers.
- The most consistently documented positive effects of teacher leadership are on the teacher leaders themselves, supporting the belief that leading and learning are interrelated. Teacher leaders grow in their understanding of instructional, professional, and organizational practices as they lead. Less empirical evidence supports student, collegial, and school-level effects. (p. 288, as cited in Blair, 2020, p. 162)

The themes that emerged from York-Barr and Duke's (2004) work validate the concerns and issues expressed by Jamaican teachers and affirm the relevance of recommendations in Table 5.1 regarding reform initiatives that are necessary for the elevation of the professional status of teachers in Jamaica.

At this point, I would be remiss if I did not acknowledge that today finds us at an almost impossible juncture in the lives of most Jamaicans. The 2020 pandemic has been devastating for Jamaica. As a country, they did not have the infrastructure to address the rampant spread of the coronavirus.

The country shut down almost immediately in March, 2020, and the tourists left. And when the tourists left, the livelihoods of most working-class Jamaicans were placed in serious peril. Individuals who depended on the tourist industry were suddenly without any source of income to pay their rents and put food on their tables. Not surprisingly, crime spread; assaults and thefts became common occurrences. As the rest of the world attempts to return to normal, Jamaicans still struggle to gain access to vaccines and attract tourists again to the island. A country that was already challenged to meet 21st century demands is now dealing with an unstable economy, crime and the continuing need to address issues related to COVID.

Schools and classrooms were shuttered in 2020 and students and teachers were forced to find alternative means to teach and learn. The Jamaican Education Transformation Commission (2022) report begins with an acknowledgement of this crisis:

> The nation now faces two crises, one long in the making and partly within our control, the other an act of God and nature that threatens mankind globally. The first is our long struggle to overcome economic stagnation and social instability. As the Most Honourable Prime Minister, Andrew Holness, recently noted in his Emancipation Day speech, this crisis is deeply rooted in our violent and exploitative colonial past. There is now general agreement that the key to overcoming it is a well-functioning system of education. It is the primary engine of social and economic growth. For individuals it generates the increased income that promotes social mobility and wellbeing; it produces the skills, knowledge, and modes of thinking our economy, polity, and social institutions need; and it promotes the values that nourish our national culture, civil society and stability. We have known this from the first day of our independence, and successive governments have, with admirable bipartisanship, devoted increasing attention and resources to its development. There is no better indication of how highly we prioritize education than the fact that, today, Jamaica is among the top 20 percent of nations in the share of its national income and annual government budget devoted to this sector. (Jamaican Education Transformation Commission, 2022, p. 1)

And so, just like educators throughout the world, Jamaicans are now struggling to define what schools will look like post-pandemic. The report (2022) added,

> The commission members have noted, COVID has magnified the many shortcomings and inequities in the system. However, the timing of the commission made it difficult to thoroughly study its impact: a full accounting is still to be known, and the data to measure its damage yet to be collected. Nonetheless, to the degree possible the Commission has tracked its influence and has recognized that, behind the devastation, there are silver lin-

ings such as the rapid learning of online teaching and the provision of internet resources. The Teaching and Curriculum committee, in particular, has also found that the crisis has led to a greater awareness and appreciation of the role of teachers and of the importance of parents, the local community and out-of-school factors for the efficient running of our schools. (Jamaican Education Transformation Commission, 2022, pp. 1–2)

Jamaican teachers who recently participated in my online graduate education classes had the following to say about teaching during the pandemic:

> I believe teachers are working above and beyond to ensure student success. More so since the pandemic. Therefore, stakeholders need to partner with teachers to gain an understanding of the magnitude of the challenges they face daily and provide the necessary support and resources. (JM8-22)

> Teachers are one of the most influential and powerful forces for equity, access and quality in education, and are key to sustainable development. However, the COVID-19 pandemic and subsequent school closures have adversely impacted them and the global education systems.... Teachers face difficulties under the current normal education system. These problems include teaching the learners where it is difficult for teachers to reach out to all the learners at home, even the teachers are using different forms of communication. It is therefore quite difficult for them to develop the skills of the learners because the learners remain at home while learning the lessons. Not all parents have the desire and ability to support their children in their studies. (JM7-22)

> While teaching is demanding, it is one of the most rewarding careers one can choose. You get to see students grow into global citizens that influence and enact change in a meaningful way. I believe teachers are generally eager to learn new ways to improve themselves. Most teachers go above and beyond the call of duty, especially during the pandemic. Teachers have provided internet services and resources for their students who lacked access during the pandemic. (JM4-22)

> Teachers have really demonstrated resilience in the pandemic and I am sure most have even surprised themselves. Many teachers had to transform their homes into offices/classrooms to facilitate online learning and the ones who also had their own biological children learning online. It is amazing how those teachers were able to balance both worlds. (JM6-22)

> I believe that teachers need to come together more within the teaching profession. It appears that teachers are just all for themselves. We need to come together more and share best practices so as to build our students while uplifting the profession. (JM5-22)

Clearly, the pandemic has challenged an already beleaguered teaching profession and a struggling educational system, but again, teachers have prevailed with characteristic optimism and a "can do spirit." Schools were already overcrowded and functioning with limited resources particularly in the area of technology, and when they were closed to cope with rising levels of COVID-19, children were sent home and families were asked to accommodate new delivery systems for education. Without additional training, wider Internet access and access to computers, it is easy to imagine the educational gaps that have emerged and the years it will take to close them.

Bettina Love (12/5/2020) recently said at a meeting of the Initiative for Race Research and Justice (Vanderbilt University), "A crisis is an amazing time to dream." And dreaming about the creation of schools and a teaching professions that is reformed and revitalized is an exciting proposition for most Jamaican educators. Arundhati Roy proposes that this moment in time may present an opportunity or a foundation for thinking about the future in new ways.

> Historically, pandemics have forced humans to break with the past and imagine their world anew. This one is no different. It is a portal, a gateway between one world and the next. We can choose to walk through it, dragging the carcasses of our prejudice and hatred, our avarice, our data banks and dead ideas, our dead rivers and smoky skies behind us. Or we can walk through lightly, with little luggage, ready to imagine another world. And ready to fight for it. (Roy, 2020, para. 48)

The word, *portal*, has multiple definitions, but the one I like for this context is the following, "a door or entrance" (Merriam-Webster Dictionary). And yes, at this momentous time in history, we have been granted a portal to the future; a door or a gate or an entrance to another world where views of schooling and education can be reconsidered and thoughtfully designed to reflect the needs of 21st century students, families and communities, and yes, even educational leaders. J. V. Gambuto (2020) begs us to consider the post-pandemic possibilities:

> From one citizen to another, I beg of you: take a deep breath, ignore the deafening noise, and think deeply about what you want to put back into your life. This is our chance to define a new version of normal, a rare and truly sacred (yes, sacred) opportunity to get rid of the bullshit and to only bring back what works for us, what makes our lives richer, what makes our kids happier, what makes us truly proud. We get to Marie Kondo the shit out of it all. We care deeply about one another. That is clear. That can be seen in every supportive Facebook post, in every meal dropped off for a neighbor, in every Zoom birthday party. We are a good people. And as a good people, we want to define—on our own terms—what this country looks like in five, 10, 50 years. This is our chance to do that, the biggest one we have ever gotten. And the best one we'll ever get. (para. 9)

His words admonish us to take advantage of the profoundness of "the great pause;" a moment for us to look around and reconsider what we are doing and ask serious questions about what we want the world to look like when this crisis passes. For Jamaican educators, these words are prophetic; what will Jamaica look like in 5, 10, 50 years? As Eldridge Cleaver argued, "You're either part of the solution, or part of the problem" (Kifner, 1998, p. 8). Returning to Roy (2020), we can use this time as a portal, "a gateway between one world and the next" or we can "choose to walk through it, dragging the carcasses of our prejudice and hatred, our avarice, our data banks and dead ideas, our dead rivers and smoky skies behind us;" the choice is ours to make (paras. 48–49).

Transformative Leadership in the 21st Century

Educational leadership in the 21st century will require that educators consider the possibilities for the future and use this opportunity or "great pause" as a chance to create school communities that attempt to accomplish things previously viewed as impossible. If we can survive a pandemic, surely we give up the shackles of preconceived notions about how we "do" schools. Or as George and Louise Spindler once suggested, we need to "question taken for granted assumptions about how we do schools" and "make the familiar strange and the strange familiar" (Spindler & Spindler, 1982, pp. 20–46). What would education and the teaching profession look like if we gave up the status quo and reinvented education and schools in a new image? Asking hard questions and refusing to accept easy answers is only a first step. Committing to a change in roles, processes and products also requires a renegotiation of how transformative change intersects with social justice initiatives. Shields (2011) helps to clarify what teacher leadership looks like when teachers commit to change that leads to school improvement and transformation of teachers' work. Transformative teacher leaders do the following:

- acknowledge power and privilege;
- articulate both individual and collective purposes (public and private good);
- deconstruct social-cultural knowledge frameworks that generate inequity and reconstruct them in more equitable ways;
- balance critique and promise;
- effect deep and equitable change;
- work towards transformation—liberation, emancipation, democracy, equity, and excellence; and
- demonstrate moral courage and activism. (p. 384)

These ideas intersect with Love's (2019) discussion of abolitionist teaching and Anderson's (2009) advocacy leadership by providing a context for teachers' work that is infused with the moral and ethical commitments inherent to teachers' work. The teachers who participated in the previously discussed study of teacher leadership in Jamaica made references to the importance of school culture in providing a context for their work. A school community that acknowledges the role of teacher beliefs and values has an opportunity to engage major stakeholders in a "naming" of the ideological orientation that informs every aspect of pedagogical planning and seek to make practice philosophically consistent. Lambert (2003a) argued that leadership capacity building is a context for changing school cultures to promote broad-based participation in the work of teachers, leaders, and learners. School cultures that openly embrace transformation as an important definition of their work support the growth and development of transformative teacher leaders. Blair (2018b) suggested,

> Transformative teacher leadership is not a panacea, but it is a way of addressing the "transformation gap" while simultaneously facilitating the growth of a profession that is professional and that has the power to not only transform school cultures, but also give birth to a transformation of teaching where teacher leadership is transformative and inclusive. Transformative teacher leaders seeking to create educational environments with high inclusion capacity could simultaneously act in the following roles:
> - intellectual leaders advocating for best practices;
> - advocates and leaders for teachers, students, and parents;
> - curriculum leaders; and
> - school–community partners and liaisons. (pp. 428–429)

As previously noted (Blair, 2018b), argued that teacher leaders working in the kinds of roles where they are regularly encouraged to be transformative leaders, have the potential to unleash the "sleeping giant" described in Katzenmeyer and Moller's (2009) work becomes a reality. Blair (2018b) described this in the following:

> Politicians and educational administrators must begin to understand the power of teacher leadership within a context of collaboration, communication and coordination of efforts.... Ultimately, this requires changes in the educational hierarchy and infrastructure where transformative leaders are rewarded and recognized and encouraged to develop progressive policies and processes that nurture the emergence of leaders at all levels—leaders will to ask difficult questions and seek inconvenient truths. (p. 426)

Understanding the role of teacher leadership in critical reconceptualizations of teachers' work is about placing teacher leadership within a context that is based on an understanding that a "new" focus must be placed on preparing for an uncertain future that has no use for nostalgia celebrating outdated models and techniques, but rather, that demands a new kind of teacher, one who is a skilled teacher and learner, but most importantly, a critical, courageous leader who is not afraid to "talk back" to individuals and groups intent on dismantling the public schools and replacing them with "choices" that ignore the democratic ideals that shaped our efforts to build schools that served the public good, not simply the "good" of a few. As John Goodlad suggested in 1988, we must prepare teachers for the schools of tomorrow, not for the schools of today. It is entirely possible that real, meaningful reform of the teaching profession where teacher leadership is the norm rather than the exception is the only hope for creating educational spaces where 21st century learners and leaders are nurtured and become active participants in challenging antiquated conceptions of education and schooling. And thus, the question that emerges is how to prepare Jamaican teachers and schools for a future that re-imagines teachers' work? It isn't productive to look at the schools of today and lament the many failures, but rather, it is imperative that we begin to disrupt previously accepted narratives about school problems and solutions. Is it acceptable to continue to issue report after report that blames teachers for the failings of schools when teachers have no voice is defining the problems and considering ways to influence change that impacts school improvement in substantive ways? Teachers' work in the 21st century must become synonymous with teacher leadership. What that looks like and how to make it happen requires a critical consideration of the many layers of complexity that shape a complicated (and political) bureaucracy.

Part of the preparation of teacher leaders for 21st century schools requires a reconsideration of how we typically think about teacher learning through professional development. References to professional development are a key part of the recommendations in the Report of the Jamaican Education Transformation Commission (2022). Professional development for which the resources and purposes remain undefined end up being random and seldom connect to the needs and concerns of teachers. Katzenmeyer and Moller (2009) suggest that with regard to planning professional development, the following questions need to be asked:

> Are adult learners, such as teacher leaders, involved in the identification of what they need to learn and in determining the process to be used for learning? This collaborative approach will likely result in increased motivation and commitment to learning.
>
> Is school-based learning that allows for transfer and application of learning to immediate workplace problems provided in the work setting?

Are teacher leaders engaged in collaborative professional development?

Is professional development for teachers sustained and ongoing through follow-up coaching and support? (p. 47)

This kind of collaboration and communication facilitates both the leadership capacity of schools and the establishment of professional learning communities that reflect the "sea change" referred to by Lambert et al. (2016); a school environment characterized by feedback spirals, propelled by reciprocal learning in community and shifts forward occurring through the dynamic of meaning-making (p. 102). In this way, they compare it to a "sea moving in upon itself." As part of this process, there is a recognition of the intertwining of both leading and learning simultaneously. Lambert (2003a) highlighted the importance of constructivists principles in teaching and learning where major stakeholders participate in the following; sharing of multiple points of view, challenging belief systems, importance of reflection and dialogue, a focus on big ideas not small pieces of information, and finally, focus on larger contexts for learning not isolated events and/or information (p. 2). The relationships and context for school culture provide ample opportunities for constructivist teachers and leaders to engage in work that promotes healthy relationships, positive interactions, and ongoing school improvement within professional learning communities.

As new definitions of teacher leadership become ingrained in our thinking about teachers' work, it is possible that 21st century schools will serve as the platform for a reconsideration of teacher's work within a context that defines both formal and informal leadership roles along a continuum that puts educational advocacy and efficacy in the "hands" of all major stakeholders, not just a few. As such, it is imperative that discussions recognize the complex relationship between the history, philosophy, and sociology of education and teacher's work as advocacy leadership. It can be argued that meaningful educational reform requires the participation of teachers who understand the impossibility of articulating a vision of *what* teacher's work should be like without first having an in-depth understanding of *why* it is that way and how critical pedagogical approaches to theory and practice can inform our thinking about the questions we must ask and the dialogues that will shape our thinking about teachers' work.

Teacher leadership cannot just be the new mantra of reformers, if it is to be more than simply another fad. It must be reinforced by real changes in the profession; changes that will support and sustain the work of teachers and the integrity of teacher knowledge. Katzenmeyer and Moller (2009) suggested that the future of teacher leadership will only be sustained if we expand career opportunities, provide adequate compensation, improve working conditions, and develop teachers who are advocates for the profession and for change (pp. 146–157). Under these conditions, I believe that schools and classrooms would change overnight into places where teacher leaders would be provided key roles in leading and directing the development of new pedagogies that support a critical analysis of schools and classrooms within the context of a new definition of the spheres of teachers' work in 21st century schools. However, while I agree with their proposal, I also believe that teachers themselves have to understand that teacher leadership for 21st century schools is something different from teacher leadership in previous decades. Teacher leadership today must include all of the earlier ideas about teacher leadership, but also take a step beyond those definitions and look to a future where teacher leadership is about teachers recreating the profession with the context of critical ideological pedagogies. It is the purpose of this book to highlight where we have been and document the possibilities and potentialities for a radical redefinition of a vision for teacher leadership as a necessary facet of teachers' work.

Oneil Madden (2022) asked the question, "should Jamaica forever remain a patty shop?" (para. 11). Interestingly, several years ago, a student made the same comparison...schools as patty shops. What does it mean? Patty shops are found on every corner in Jamaica and patties are cheap. Everyone eats patties although most would agree they are not healthy, but they are sustenance for the masses. And therein may lay the similarity to schools. Public schools serve the masses an educational system that is seldom notable, but rather, is cheap and simply "feeds" the people a steady diet of a "one size fits all" approach to teaching and learning; there is nothing gourmet about Jamaican public schools. Madden adds, "We cannot want First World-type education when we have these deficiencies in the system" (para. 11), and yet, he questions whether anyone takes seriously the need to upgrade and make Jamaican teachers and schools comparable to other nations. Again, the notion of a patty shop brings up images of "side of the road," shoddy standards, basic sustenance, short-term gratification but no long-term benefits. Even the people who operate a patty shop are semi-skilled and simply getting by with minimum training and expertise. Does the metaphor reflect a belief that teachers have more in common with the operators of patty shops than other professionals, like doctors and lawyers? If Jamaicans view schools as patty shops, does this belief impact perceptions regarding the viability of school improvement efforts and the future of teacher leadership? Can patty shop owners be the face of teacher leadership? Probably not, and so again, we are back to the question of how we change perceptions. How do we re-imagine teacher leadership and school improvement in the 21st century in Jamaican schools if patty shops are a commonly accepted metaphor for the public schools?

New ways of thinking about Jamaican teachers' work must include situating teacher leadership and professional learning communities into renewed and revised definitions of 21st century schools. The ideas in this book provide a foundation for teacher efforts to take back control of their professional lives and begin the process of redirecting the progress of the profession within a larger theoretical framework; a framework that recognizes that the emergence of teachers with a critical, purposeful consciousness of themselves as workers in hegemonic institutions will represent the beginning of substantive efforts to reform the schools on behalf of students and teachers. A stronger teaching profession will emerge when teachers are recognized (and supported) as political actors with responsibility for advocating on behalf of social justice and the propagation of schools that seriously consider how to meet their moral and ethical commitments to the students they serve; *every child can learn, every child must learn.* In 2004, the Task Force on Educational Reform Final Report, *Jamaica, A Transformed Education System,* described strategies for "achieving the vision through transformation.... the difference between the 'current path' and the 'transformation path' is the transformation gap, which we must close" (p. 65). In this book, I propose that teacher leaders are the key to closing this gap and making schools more accommodating to multiple visions of how schools are organized to promote higher levels of school improvement. As one of the participants in the teacher leadership study indicated, "Teachers are the cornerstone of a society" (JM7-22). A failure to include teacher leaders and their voices into the tapestry of school reform efforts will yield another round of blame and shame as school improvement efforts continue to document mounting failures in achievement and Jamaican children lose out on opportunities to take their rightful places as 21st century global citizens. This is the opportunity for educational leaders stretching from the Ministry to individual schools to take seriously efforts to transcend previously narrow definitions of teacher's work and participate in the shaping of a new vision for Jamaican schools and Jamaican teachers—a vision that reflects the unique needs and concerns of Jamaican citizens. Inclusive to this vision will be the creation of public spaces that facilitate critical dialogue and discussion about the creation of educational sites that are amenable to meaningful and substantive school improvement efforts and the redefinition of teachers' roles and responsibilities for shaping 21st century Jamaican schools. Consider the following questions:

1. What is uniquely Jamaican about Jamaican education? Is that reflected in schools and classrooms? In teachers' work? In policies, processes, and products?
2. What does a reimagined teaching profession look like in Jamaica? Think about specifics. Define the problems? What has to change? What are the obstacles to change?
3. Is Jamaica ready to reimagine schools and teachers' work in new images?
4. What changes occurred during the Pandemic that will impact schools in the future? Good? Bad?
5. What are the obstacles to "disrupting the current narrative" about teacher leadership?

References

Acker-Hocevar, M., & Touchton, D. (1999, April). *A model of power as social relationship: Teacher leaders describe the phenomena of effective agency on practice* [Paper presentation]. American Educational Research Association Annual Meeting, Montreal, Quebec, Canada. https://eric.ed.gov/?q=acker-hocevar+and+touchton&id=ED456108

Acker-Hocevar, M., Cruz-Janzen, M. I., & Wilson, C. L. (2012). *Leadership from the ground up: Effective schooling in traditionally low performing schools.* Information Age Publishing.

Anderson, G. (2009). *Advocacy Leadership: Toward a post-reform agenda in education.* Routledge.

Berry, B. (2019). Teacher leadership: Prospects and promises. *The Kappan, 100*(7), 49–55.

Bissessar, C. (2017). *Assessing the current state of education in the Caribbean.* IGI Global.

Blair, E. J. (2018a). *By the light of the silvery moon: Teacher moonlighting and the dark side of teachers' work.* Myers Education Press.

Blair, E. J. (2018b). Transformative teacher leadership is inclusive education. In D. A. Conrad & S. N. J. Blackman (Eds.), *Responding to learner diversity and learning difficulties.* Information Age Publishing.

Blair, E. J. (2020). Teacher leadership in the United States. In E. Blair, C. Roofe, & S. Timmins (Eds.), *A cross cultural consideration of teacher leaders' narratives of power, agency and school culture: England, Jamaica and the United States* (pp. 117–167). Myers Education Press.

Blair, E., & Williams, K. (2021). *The handbook on Caribbean education.* Information Age Publishing.

Brown, M. M. (1992). Caribbean first year teacher's reasons for choosing teaching as a career. *Journal of Education for Teaching, 18*(2), 185–195.

Brown, R. (2004). *School culture and organization: Lessons from research and experience.* Paper for the Denver Commission on Secondary School Reform, Denver, CO.

Bissessar, C. (2017). Professionalism among Jamaican educators: Principles, practices, and the practitioner's perspectives. In *Assessing the current state of education in the Caribbean* (pp. 24–45). IGI Global.

Center for Strengthening the Teaching Profession. (2009). *Teacher leadership skills framework.* https://cstp-wa.org/teacher-leadership/teacher-leadership-skills-framework

Covey, S. (1982). *The 7 habits of highly successful people: Powerful lessons in personal change.* Simon & Schuster.

Cunningham, S. (2014, August 21). NEI Report: More schools failing. *The Gleaner.* https://jamaica-gleaner.com/article/lead-stories/20140821/nei-report-more-schools-failing

Danielson, C. (2006). *Teacher leadership that strengthens professional practice.* Association for Supervision and Curriculum Development.

Davis, R. (2004). *Task force on educational reform: A transformed education system.*

Emdin, C. (2018, March 6). *Teaching and being ratchetdemic* [video]. YouTube. https://www.youtube.com/watch?v=4QmFREcXri0

Etzioni, A. (Ed.). (1969). *The semi-professions and their organizations: Teachers, nurses, and social workers.* Free Press.

Evans, H. (2001). *Inside Jamaican schools.* University Press of the West Indies.

Evans, H. (2006). *Inside Hillview High School: An ethnography of an urban Jamaican school.* University Press of the West Indies.

Fix Our Broke and Broken Education System. (2016, January 21). *The Gleaner.* https://jamaica-gleaner.com/article/lead-stories/20160124/fix-our-broke-and-broken-education-system

Freire, P. (1973). *Education for critical consciousness.* Seabury Press.

Freire, P. (1985). *The politics of education: Culture, power and liberation.* Macmillan.

Freire, P. (2000). *Pedagogy of the oppressed* (30th anniversary edition). Continuum.

Freire, P. (2007). *Daring to dream.* Paradigm.

Gambuto, J. V. (2020, April 10). *Prepare for the ultimate gaslighting.* Forge–Medium. https://forge.medium.com/prepare-for-the-ultimate-gaslighting-6a8ce3f0a0e0

Giroux, H. A. (1988). *Teachers as intellectuals: Toward a critical pedagogy of learning.* Praeger.

Giroux, H. A. (2012). *Education and the crisis of public values: Challenging the assault on teachers, students, & public education.* Peter Lang Publishers.

Goodlad, J. (1988). *A place called school.* McGraw Hill.

Graham, G. (2012). *Race and class interaction in Jamaica—and its impact on the world.* Jamaicans.com. https://jamaicans.com/raceandclassinjamaica/

Hall, S. (1980). *Culture, media, language.* Routledge.

Hamilton, M. (1997). The availability and sustainability of educational opportunities for Jamaican female students: A historical overview. In E. Leo-Rynie, B. Bailey, & C. Barrow (Eds.), *Gender: A Caribbean multidisciplinary perspective* (pp. 133–143). Ian Randle.

Heremuru Dsl, C. G. (2013). *Building Jamaica through education: The way forward.* Outskirts Press.

Hill-Berry, N. (2017). Professionalism among Jamaican educators: Principles, practices, and the practitioners' perspectives. In C. Bissessar (Ed.), *Assessing the current state of education in the Caribbean.* IGI Global.

Hines, H. (2021, August 19). Teachers are fed up. *Jamaica Observer.* https://www.jamaicaobserver.com/news/teachers-are-fed-up/

Hutchinson, B. (2021, November 24). Teachers not greedy! *The Gleaner.* https://www.jamaicaobserver.com/news/teachers-not-greedy/

Ingersoll, R. M., & Collins, G. J. (2018). The status of teaching as a profession. In J. Ballantine, J. Spade, & J. Stuber (Eds.), *Schools and society: A sociological approach to education* (6th ed.; pp. 199–213) Pine Forge Press/SAGE.

Ingersoll, R. M., & Merrill, E. (2011). The status of teaching as a profession. In J. Ballantine & J. Spade (Eds.), *Schools and society: A sociological approach to education* (4th ed.; pp. 185–189). Pine Forge Press/SAGE.

Jamaica Teaching Council (2022). *About JTC.* https://jtc.gov.jm/300f0-web-agency-home-2/

Jamaica: Teaching Profession. (n.d.). StateUniversity.com Education Encyclopedia. https://education.stateuniversity.com/pages/733/Jamaica-TEACHING-PROFESSION.html

Jamaican Education Transformation Commission. (2022). *The reform of education in Jamaica, 2021: Abridged version.* Report of the Jamaica Education Transformation Commission.

Johnson, S. (2022a, March 11). *Every child can learn, every child must learn? Part I.* https://jamaica-gleaner.com/article/lifestyle/20220311/every-child-can-learn-every-child-must-learn-part-1

Johnson, S. (2022b, March 18). *Every child can learn, every child must learn? Part II.* https://jamaica-gleaner.com/article/lifestyle/20220318/every-child-can-learn-every-child-must-learn-part-ii

Katzenmeyer, M., & Moller, G. (2009). *Awakening the sleeping giant: Helping teachers develop as leaders* (3rd ed.). Corwin Press.

Kifner, J. (1998, May 2). Eldridge Cleaver, Black Panther who became G.O.P. conservative, is dead at 62. *The New York Times,* B, p. 8. https://www.nytimes.com/1998/05/02/us/eldridge-cleaver-black-panther-who-became-gop-conservative-is-dead-at-62.html

King, N. (2001, May 17). Caribbean teacher recruitment for New York City schools is a big success. *Queens Chronicle.* https://www.qchron.com/caribbean-teacher-recruitment-for-new-york-city-schools-is-a-big-success/article_722cdfb7-81d9-5955-9abc-b08d40ea7e57.html

Lambert, L. (2003a). *Leadership capacity for lasting school improvement.* Association for Supervision and Curriculum Development.

Lambert, L. (2003b). Leadership redefined: An evocative context for teacher leadership. *School Leadership & Management, 23*(4), 421–430. Carfax Publishing, Taylor & Francis Group.

Lambert, L., Zimmerman, D. P., & Gardner, M. E. (2016). *Liberating leadership capacity: Pathways for educational wisdom.* Teachers College Press.

Levin, B., & Schrum, L. (2017). *Every teacher a leader: Developing the needed dispositions, knowledge, and skills for teacher leadership.* Corwin.

Lewis, A. (2022, May 7). JTA head blasts gov't over low wages. *The Gleaner.* https://www.jamaicaobserver.com/news/jta-head-again-blasts-govt-over-low-wages

Lewis, J. (2018, June 17). Do not get lost in a sea of despair. Be hopeful, be optimistic. Our struggle is not the struggle of a day, a week, a month, or a year, it is the struggle of a lifetime. Never, ever be afraid to make some noise and get in good trouble, necessary trouble. [Tweet]. Twitter. https://twitter.com/repjohnlewis/status/1011991303599607808

Little, J. W. (1988). Assessing the prospects for teacher leadership. In A. Lieberman (Ed.), *Building a professional culture in schools* (pp. 78–106). Teachers College Press.

Lortie, D. (1969). The balance of control and autonomy in elementary school teaching. In A. A. Etzioni (Ed.), *The semi-professions and their organizations: Teachers, nurses and social workers* (pp. 1–53). Free Press.

Lortie, D. (1975). *School teacher.* University of Chicago Press.

Love, B. L. (2019). *We want to do more than survive: Abolitionist teaching and the pursuit of educational freedom.* Beacon Press.

Love, B. L. (2020, December 5). *Racial justice in education and society virtual conference* [Presentation]. Initiative for Race Research and Justice, Vanderbilt Peabody College, Nashville, TN.

Madden, O. (2022, May 17). *Jamaican Teaching Council Bill: A necessary piece of legislation.* https://www.jamaicaobserver.com/columns/jamaica-teaching-council-bill-a-necessary-piece-of-legislation/

Meighoo, K. (1999). Curry goat a metaphor for the Indian/Jamaican future. *Social and Economic Studies, 48*(3), 43–59. Sir Arthur Lewis Institute of Social and Economic Studies. https://www.jstor.org/stable/27865148

Merriam-Webster Dictionary. (n.d.). Portal. In *Merriam-Webster Online Dictionary.* Retrieved September 19, 2022, from https://www.merriam-webster.com/dictionary/portal

Miller, P. (2013). *School leadership in the Caribbean: Perceptions, practices, paradigms.* Symposium Books.

Ministry of Education. (2004). *Task force on educational reform. A transformed education system.*

Ministry of Education Youth and Culture. (2004). *The development of education: National report of Jamaica.*

National Report of Jamaica by the Planning and Development Division. (2008). *Development of Education.* Ministry of Education.

Noel, K. (2009). Education reform. *The Gleaner.* https://old.jamaica-gleaner.com/gleaner/20090522/cleisure/cleisure3.html

Oren, T. (2021, May 5). *Many years ago, I was walking around a vacant lot in New Kingston that would later become Emancipation Park. During* [Facebook post]. Facebook. https://www.facebook.com/tom.oren.92

Ornstein, A. C. (1977). Teachers as professionals. *Social Science, 52*(3), 139–144. https://www.jstor.org/stable/41886173

Parham, J. N., & Gordon, S. P. (2011). Moonlighting: A harsh reality for many teachers. *The Kappan, 92*(5), 47–51.

Planning and Development Division. (2008). *The development of education: National report of Jamaica.* Ministry of Education.

Planning Institute of Jamaica. (2010). *Vision 2030 Jamaica National Development Plan: Planning for a secure and prosperous future.* The Herald Limited.

Roofe, C. (2020). Teacher leadership in Jamaica. In E. Blair, C. Roofe, & S. Timmins (Eds.), *A cross cultural consideration of teacher leaders' narratives of power, agency and school culture: England, Jamaica and the United States* (pp. 63–107). Myers Education Press.

Roy, A. (2020, April 3). The pandemic is a portal. *Financial Times.* https://www.ft.com/content/10d8f5e8-74eb-11ea-95fe-fcd274e920ca

Saunders, A. (2020, February 14). Schools lose. *Jamaica Observer.* https://www.jamaicaobserver.com/news/schools-lose/

Sherlock, P., & Bennett, H. (1998). *The story of the Jamaican people.* Markus Wiener.

Shields, C. (2011). *Transformative leadership: A reader.* Peter Lang Publishing.

Silva, D. Y., Gimbert, B., & Nolan, J. (2000). Sliding the doors: Locking and unlocking possibilities for teacher leadership. *Teachers College Record, 102*(4), 779–804. https://doi.org/10.1111/0161-4681.00077

Silvera, J. (2011, March 27). Used and abused teachers recruited to work in New York cry foul. *The Gleaner.* https://jamaicagleaner.com/gleaner/20110327/lead/lead1.html

Silvera, J. (2022, March 10). No mass exodus of teachers says Williams. *The Gleaner.* https://jamaica-gleaner.com/article/lead-stories/20220310/no-mass-exodus-teachers-says-williams

Sizer, T. (2004). *Horace's compromise: The dilemma of the American high school.* Harper.

Spindler, G., & Spindler, L. (1982). Roger Harker and Schoenhausen: From familiar to strange and back again. In G. Spindler (Ed.), *Doing the ethnography of schooling: Educational anthropology in action* (pp. 20–46). Holt, Rinehart, and Winston.

Szczesiul, S. A., & Huizenga, J. L. (2015). Building structure and agency: Exploring the role of teacher leadership in teacher collaboration. *Journal of School Leadership, 25*(2), 364-410. https://doi.org/10.1177/105268461502500207

Task Force on Educational Reform Final Report. (2004). *Jamaica: A transformed education system.* https://jis.gov.jm/estp/docs/Reports/JA%20Education%20Reform%20TaskForce%202004.pdf

Turriff, C. (2002, March 22). Jamaica debates 'Queen's English.' *The Daily Guardian.* https://www.theguardian.com/education/2002/mar/22/tefl

Tyack, D., & Cuban, L. (1995). *Tinkering with utopia: A century of public school reform.* Harvard University Press.

University of West Indies. (2022). UWI School of Education-Jamaica Teaching Council Act, 2022 at the Joint Select Committee. https://www.mona.uwi.edu/soe/soe/humed/uwi-school-education-jamaica-teaching-council-act-2022-joint-select-committee

Wehling, B. (2007). Foreword. In B. Wehling (Ed.), *Building a 21st century U.S. education system* (pp. 13–21). National Commission on Teaching and America's Future.

Weiler, K. (1988). *Women teaching for change: Gender, class and power.* Bergin & Garvey.

Williams, S., & Staulters, M. (2010). Literacy instruction in rural elementary schools in Jamaica: Response to professional development. *The Journal of Negro Education, 79*(2), 97–111.

Winkler, A. C. (1995). *Going home to teach.* LMH Publishing.

Wray, S. (2022, February 8). *JTA agrees to 4% wage increase despite some reservations.* Nationwide Radio JM. https://nationwideradiojm.com/jta-agrees-to-4-wage-increase-despite-some-reservations/

York-Barr, J., & Duke, K. (2004). What do we know about teacher leadership? Findings from two decades of scholarship. *Review of Educational Research, 74*(3), 255–316. https://doi.org/10.3102/00346543074003255

Index

A

abolitionist teaching, 56–57, 83
accountability, x, xvi, 3–4, 6, 9, 11, 23, 41, 47, 67
action research: teacher leaders and, 53
advocacy leadership, 57, 83, 85
Anderson, Garth, 39–40
Anderson, Gary: advocacy leadership and, 57, 83

B

banking concept of education: Paulo Freire and, 41–43
begin with the end in mind: Stephen Covey and, xxi, 1, 25

C

challenges: social and economic, 16–19
colonialism, xv, xviii, 12–13
constructivism, 55; teacher leaders and, 53, 85
Covey, Stephen: *begin with the end in mind* and, xxi, 1, 25
curried goat: Jamaican identity and, 2

D

diversity: role of, 1–12

E

Education and the crisis of public values: Challenging the assault on teachers, students, and public education (Giroux), xix, 74–75
Emdin, Christopher, 71–72
Evans, Hyacinth, 49–50; *Inside Jamaican Schools* and, 7, 18, 40, 43, 49–50; *Inside Hillview High School: An Ethnography of an Urban Jamaican School* and, 7
every child can learn, every child must learn, 6, 13–25, 87

F

Freire, Paulo, xxi, 41; teacher-student relationships and, 41–43, 49–50

G

Gardner, Solomon, xvi
Giroux, Henry: *Education and the crisis of public values: Challenging the assault on teachers, students, and public education* and, xix, 74–75
Going Home to Teach (Winkler), xviii, 18–19
Graham, George, xvii, 2, 17–18

H

Holness, Andrew, 6
Horace's Compromise (Sizer), 16
how we define the problem determines the solution, 5, 9, 35, 73

I

Inside Hillview High School: An ethnography of an urban Jamaican school (Evans), 7
Inside Jamaican schools (Evans), 7, 18, 40, 43, 49–50

J

Jamaica: culture and, xvii–xix, 1–12; identity and, 1–12; patty shops and, 86; schools and, xix–xx, 13–25; teacher voices and, 23, 36–47, 59–70; teachers and, 3–4, 27–47
Jamaican Education Transformation Commission, 5–7, 11, 19–20, 41, 79–80, 84
Jamaican Teachers' Association (JTA), 3, 8, 29, 47, 77
Jamaica Teacher Council (JTC), 39
Jamaica Teaching Council Bill (2022), 38

L

leadership capacity, 54–55, 83
Love, Bettina, 13, 81; abolitionist teaching and, 56–57, 83

M

Meighoo, Kirk: Jamaican identity and, 2
Ministry of Education and Youth (MOEY), 38–39, 47, 77
Ministry of Education, Youth, and Information (MOEYI), 5, 8, 12–15, 19–20

O

oppression, xv, xviii, 12, 34, 42–43
out of many, one people, xviii, 2, 12, 14, 17

P

pandemic: impact of, 8; teachers and, 76–82
patty shops: education and, 86
Planning Institute of Jamaica, 10
principals: role of, 54
professional development, xv, 3–4, 6, 9, 23, 41, 52, 84–85
professional learning communities (PLC), 55, 87; sea change and, 85

Q

Queen's English, 21

R

race, xv, xvii–xviii, 14, 18–19

S

Samuda, Karl, 29
school improvement: influencing activity and, 51–52; sustainability and, 56
schools: culture and, 56, 60–63, 83, 85; history of, 13–15; reform and, 5–7, 19–20
semi-profession: teachers and, xx, 8, 10, 21, 34, 47, 50, 75. *See also* teachers
Sizer, Theodore: *Horace's Compromise* and, 16
skin color: impact of, xv
Smith, Winston: Jamaican Teachers' Association and, 3, 29–30
social class, xv–xvi, xviii, 16, 50
social justice, xv, xvii, 12, 17, 20, 41, 50–51, 60, 66–69, 77, 82, 87
sustainability, 56

T

Task Force on Educational Reform (2004), 13, 15, 20, 37–39, 87
teacher leaders, 50–59; advocacy and, 85; constructivist learners and, 53, 55, 85; decision-making and, 63–65; definitions of, 50–59, 85; dispositions of, 51; pandemic and, 76–82; power and advocacy and, 66–70; sleeping giant of, 52–53, 83; sustainability and, 56; work and expertise of, 65–66, 72–74; ZRESS and, 41, 60
teachers: compensation and, 29–30; conditions of work and, 9; developmental model for, 57–58; leadership and, 7–12, 42, 50–59; moonlighting and, 31–36; political acts and, 57; professionalism and, 46–47, 75–76; public good and, 73; semi-profession and, xx, 8, 10, 21, 23, 47, 50, 75; transformative intellectuals as, 74–75; voices of, 23, 36–47, 59–70; work and, 4–5, 7–12. *See also* Jamaica
The Development of Education, National Report of Jamaica, 38–39
The Reform of Education in Jamaica, 2021, 5–7, 19–20, 41
Thwaites, Ronald, 23
transformation gap, 87
transformative teacher leadership, 56, 74–75, 82–87
Twenty-first century: digital world and, 8; educational leadership and, xx–xxi, 49–70; global economy and, 6; teaching profession and, 9; transformative leadership in, 82–87

U

universal education: tenets of, 23

V

Vision 2030 Jamaica National Development Plan: Planning for a secure and prosperous future, 10–11

W

Williams, Fayval, 29, 30
Winkler, Anthony: *Going Home to Teach* and, xviii, 18–19, 21

Z

ZRESS: teacher leaders and, 41, 60

CPSIA information can be obtained
at www.ICGtesting.com
Printed in the USA
JSHW030538130223
37636JS00001B/2